D0802103

EMBRACING
THE AWKWARD

For permission requests, please contact the publisher at:

Mango Publishing Group
2850 Douglas Road, 3rd Floor
Coral Gables, FL 33134 U.S.A.
info@mango.bz

For special orders, quantity sales, course adoptions and corporate sales, please email the publisher at sales@mango.bz. For trade and wholesale sales, please contact Ingram Publisher Services at: customer.service@ingramcontent.com or +1.800.509.4887.

Embracing the Awkward: A Guide for Teens to Succeed at School, Life, and Relationships

Library of Congress Cataloging
ISBN: (p) 978-1-63353-736-1, (e) 978-1-63353-737-8
Library of Congress Control Number: 2018937946
BISAC - YAN051110 YOUNG ADULT NONFICTION / Social Topics / Friendship
BISAC - YAN051200 YOUNG ADULT NONFICTION / Social Topics / Self-
        Esteem & Self-Reliance

Printed in the United States of America

EMBRACING THE AWKWARD

A Guide for Teens to Succeed at School, Life, and Relationships

JOSHUA RODRIGUEZ

Mango Publishing

CORAL GABLES, FL

 mango

To my parents; the loving support system I needed for all the crazy dreams I've tried to pursue growing up. To my wife, who inspires me to be a leader, a caregiver, a husband and a friend. And to anyone that is ready to be their best self and show the world that they can be somebody great.

CONTENTS

Awkward

Ôk-wərd

Adjective

Causing difficulty; hard to do or deal with.
Ungraceful; clumsy.

Synonyms: difficult, tricky, uncomfortable, unpleasant

INTRODUCTION

"OUR PRIME PURPOSE IN THIS LIFE IS TO HELP OTHERS. AND IF YOU CAN'T HELP THEM, AT LEAST DON'T HURT THEM." –DALAI LAMA

UNDERSTANDING YOURSELF AND YOUR PURPOSE

"Life is tough, *ruff ruff ruff*." These are the words that came to me once in a dream. I dreamed that I was standing on an empty street—the sky was cloudy, the air chilled my skin, and all that stood in front of me was a small, unfamiliar dog. The dog slowly approached, as curious of me as I was of him, and said those words to me as I bent down to pet him. It was an odd dream to have—one that I don't really understand even to this day—but the impression it left on me has helped shape every major decision I've ever had to make.

Sometimes in life our environment can be daunting or uncomfortable, our decisions tough, and the outcomes even tougher. But knowing who we are, and that we are not alone in our journey, can sometimes make all the difference.

If you are alive (you probably are if you're reading this), then you will one day question your purpose. It's OK, everyone does. So, how do you know what it is? How do you know how to find it? You should start by looking within yourself. Knowing yourself, your values, and your strengths can all help you deal with any mishaps, curve balls, awkward moments, or complete disasters that will one day come your way.

There are plenty of days where I question what my purpose is, whether I've made the right decisions, and if I've followed the right path. But what I've come to really understand about purpose, about *my* purpose, is that it's constantly redefined every single day.

From the moment we wake up to the moment we go to sleep, what lies ahead of us is every opportunity imaginable. And while that might sound a bit idealistic (and trust me, it is), **believing that we can do anything stops us from creating limitations that aren't there to begin with**.

If I woke up tomorrow and decided that today is the day that I will help someone, whether by rushing into a burning building to save their life or taking a moment to listen to them vent, I can fulfill my purpose in the biggest or smallest of ways because I know I will feel fulfilled as I do it. So what is *my* purpose then? Right now, as I see it, I want to live my life in such a way that I am helpful and compassionate toward myself and others, mindful of my behaviors, words, and feelings, and confident in my ability to be somebody great.

And while that last sentence may seem like I have it all figured out, I simply don't. I struggle too, just like you do, because life *is* tough. No matter how much you try, you will always hit barriers along the way. Am I hanging out with friends who are going to help me excel in life? Should I choose a different major in college because it might be easier for me to get a job? Is this the right person for me, the one I want to spend my life with? Life will always feed you new questions, and as you sort yourself out and try to answer them, your purpose may change from day to day.

So, is it all just one big windy road that you have no control over? It can be if you don't establish a grounding in what it is that makes you great. Knowing what my values are and working hard to carry them forward in every step I take is what helps keep me on track. While the world around me continues to throw questions, I *know* I can handle anything despite any challenges and awkward situations that lie ahead.

Having this in *your* life can also do the same for you. Values ground us in what kind of people we are, how we have grown, and how we choose to act in the world. Having such an important foundation can give you a sense of purpose all by itself. Also, it leads you to one of the most important results of knowing who you are: confidence.

Everyone goes through uncomfortable or awkward moments or phases in their lives. During these times, being confident and secure in yourself isn't always easy, especially when growing up. Growing up is the time when we develop our identities and learn the most about ourselves and the world. Also, did I mention life can be tough? Any new situation or challenge can understandably be intimidating.

But how you approach a person, situation, or challenge will make all the difference in how it turns out (as well as in how you experience it). Stepping into new situations with confidence—coming from your sense of purpose and knowing who you are—can help you turn something new and awkward into a learning experience. So instead of cringing at yourself when you make the wrong decision, fail your test, say the wrong thing to your crush, or bomb your first job interview—let your inner confidence and purpose help you embrace the awkward.

MY PURPOSE GROWING UP

When I was a young boy growing up, I always felt like I needed to work hard to stand out as my own individual self. Being the middle child of three boys meant there was a lot of butting heads and competing for everything from toys to sleeping on the top bunk of the bunk bed. Normally the middle child gets the stigma of feeling left out or overlooked, but that wasn't really the case with me. In fact, I think it actually pushed me to work harder to establish myself so that I could be proud of who I was by just being myself.

In my house, my brothers and I had a pretty interesting dynamic with one another. My older brother, who is one year my senior, carried himself as a bit of a leader, always the first to make a decision and to try new things because he was the firstborn. My younger brother, who is three years my junior, strove a little more to be accepted by the two of us; because of the bigger age difference, it was harder for him to be able to do the same things we wanted to do. Because of all of this, I feel like I learned early on what each of their different needs were and how to peacefully make everyone happy. For example, one Christmas, I remember our parents buying us each a WWF action figure. When we opened them up, my older brother proclaimed that he had been given the best figure and showed it off to the two of us, so I joined in his excitement to make him feel happy with what he got. When my younger brother and I opened our figures, I saw that I had one that he would have liked more. Just seeing the expression of disappointment on his face made me realize that although I didn't care about the character he had, I knew he would be happier with mine, so I traded with him. My older brother was happy, my younger brother was happy, and I was happy that they both felt the love and respect they needed in that moment.

It started to become clear to me that doing the right thing and helping others made me feel good about myself; knowing I could make small sacrifices that didn't hurt me long-term made me realize that there was something to humility and sacrifice.

When I started going to school, my parents instilled in me the importance of doing well academically, so I made it my mission once again to aim to work hard so I would stand out. I remember in elementary school, I would try my best to win as many awards, certificates, and plaques as possible, I even had a bit of a feud going with another girl in my class over this. She had the same dedication and drive as I did to succeed to the best of her abilities, so we both made sure to enter every contest, write every essay, and create every art project possible just so we could be recognized for our achievements. During one awards ceremony in the fourth grade, the two of us were called up to the stage so many times that we decided to stand in the aisles instead of sitting down, just in case we were called up again. It was an adrenaline rush for me to be recognized for my achievements, I knew that deep down inside that this was exactly what my parents wanted from me, and the last thing I ever wanted to do was let them down.

Once I reached middle school, that started to change a little bit. The kids I hung out with weren't bad, but they certainly didn't make it easy to uphold my perfect student image. We pulled lots of pranks on each other without any regard for how they could get us into serious trouble. Whether it was jumping across the lunch tables or having wrestling matches in class, I had quite of a bit of explaining to do to my parents whenever they got a call from the school. In some ways, a lot of it was harmless fun, but one thing I knew was never to do anything that would get me in serious trouble. Nothing scared me more than getting suspended or expelled from school. If I ever met that fate, I would have had no clue how to explain it to my parents.

By high school, I was so set in my ways of never letting my parents down that I avoided anything that my parents told me not to do. When my friends started drinking and smoking, I turned it all down because I knew my parents wouldn't be happy with me. If some of my friends were cutting class or ditching school, I told them I couldn't do that because I wasn't allowed to. By the end of the year, I had even been awarded the perfect attendance award, along with four other kids who seemed equally as obedient as I was. What's also interesting is that my parents weren't super strict with me at all. They laid down ground rules but were very nonchalant about enforcing them. I think what was really happening with me was that my sense of worth and acceptance was completely tied to how well I did and what they would think of me. I didn't spend a lot of time asking myself what my purpose was simply because it had been laid out very clearly—do what your parents say and make them proud.

ONE QUESTION IN COLLEGE THAT CHANGED EVERYTHING

•

"YOU WILL NEVER BE HAPPY IF YOU CONTINUE TO SEARCH FOR WHAT HAPPINESS CONSISTS OF. YOU WILL NEVER LIVE IF YOU ARE LOOKING FOR THE MEANING OF LIFE."

–ALBERT CAMUS

•

Things seemed to be going extremely well for me until I started college. Just like in school during the years before college, I relied on my parents to help me define my path so I could know exactly what I had to do to succeed. When it came time to pick my major, I really had no clue what to focus on. I had lots of different interests at the time, but no clear direction to follow, so I asked my parents what I should do. Since I enjoyed designing in Photoshop and creating websites, my parents suggested I go into the computer engineering field. I thought that made sense, so I took their lead and signed up for physics and math my first semester there.

I knew things were going to suck from the very first day of classes. I had set my alarm clock to a radio station, thinking that would be the perfect thing to wake up to in the morning. The very next day at 8:00 AM, I heard a Backstreet Boys song start to play as I woke up, sang along in my head, and then drifted back to sleep. When I woke up again, it was already 10:30 AM, and not only had I missed my physics class, I was already halfway into my math class. I rushed out of my room and ran to class, thinking to myself, *I can't screw up this early on, I just can't.* Waking up late that morning ended up being the least of my problems, however; as I dove deeper into learning physics and math, I realized I just couldn't keep up. The topics and material we were covering were not only too hard for me, I felt so disconnected from the class that I just felt sick to my stomach about going. Was computer engineering the right major for me? Had I made the right decision here?

I had never been steered wrong before when I followed my parents' lead, so why did this all feel so wrong to me? By the end of the first semester, I was placed on academic probation for getting below a 2.0 GPA. I received an F in my physics class and got a D in my math class, which left me wondering if college was right for me. Deep down, I wanted to be there, but I knew something had to change. I felt depressed, I felt worthless, and worst of all, I felt like I was disappointing my parents. So early one morning, when my roommate had left for the weekend, I woke up early on a Saturday, opened the shades to the room to let in the sunlight, and then asked myself the most complex question I'd ever asked: why should I go on living, and what is my purpose for being alive?

I told myself that if I couldn't find an answer by the end of the day, then I would simply end it. I couldn't imagine a life without a purpose.

I sat there for hours, thinking and thinking about what I could do and what my purpose was, and it wasn't until later in that evening that the answer finally hit me. My purpose in life is to experience it, and the reason I should go on living is to share it with others. I felt like the answer was so incredibly simple, yet it was something I had never thought about before. For my second semester of college, I knew I had to break from my current path. I needed to define for myself what success would look like, and I needed to do it for one person: me. I changed my college major to "undecided" and enrolled in philosophy classes to start from the ground up on recognizing how I could create a path for my new purpose.

That wasn't the only thing that changed for me, though; as time went on, I suddenly became more open to the world around me. I started to notice the squirrels running by on the grass, the way the sun set over the buildings on campus, and how each and every person was someone just like me, trying to find a way to be somebody great. I felt connected with everyone and everything, and I knew at that point more than ever that I didn't have to make my life revolve around someone else's approval, I just had to live it for me.

DON'T STOP WHEN THINGS ARE GOOD

•

"PASSION IS AN UNMATCHED FUEL. ADD BEING HAPPY TO THAT AND YOU HAVE A WONDERFUL FORMULA FOR GOOD HEALTH."

–GARY VAYNERCHUK

•

By the time I graduated college, I had already been working part-time at an internship that took me on full-time once I had my bachelor's degree in Business Marketing and Digital Arts. I felt accomplished—I had secured a job when so many of the people around me were struggling to find something to do, and I finally felt like I had made it. At first, I was excited to be working where I did, at a technology company that sold tech products to college bookstores. I was in charge of managing the website, adding products, designing campaigns, and more. And while it definitely was fun for the first year, I slowly began to realize that it wasn't exactly what I wanted to do.

Those were feelings I was quick to dismiss though; there were lots of people struggling to find a job in the first place, who was I to be complaining about having a job I didn't like? So I instead decided to shift my focus to doing things outside of my job, thinking I had to dedicate forty hours of my week to someone else just so I could live for the weekends. It was the type of reality that I figured was normal and expected once you graduate. Little did I realize I was back in the same trap as before, I was working to meet the expectations of others and not those of myself.

I had become complacent, living day to day for someone else's goals and dreams and not my own. And the reason I never did anything about it was because I had learned how to fit my life around it; it was like a giant rock in the road that I would just drive around because I never wanted to move it. In some ways it really didn't work for me, but in other ways it was completely comforting to know that I had security there. Year after year, I remained at that job with no plans for growth in my career or for my future. I was so sucked into the day-to-day that I never took the time to think beyond that.

I was at that job for four years before the company let me go. The reason they let me go was because they were going to outsource my job to someone else to do it for cheaper, and honestly, that was probably the best thing that could have ever happened to me. I remember the day my boss called me and my coworker who also worked on the website into her office and told us the "bad" news. I smiled at her, thanked her for hiring me, and suddenly felt like the world was completely open to me. I had never seen the world around me like this before, I felt like if I applied myself where I needed to, I could literally accomplish anything.

I called my mom on the way back home and explained what had happened with such a sense of relief. Had I not had the rock moved for me, who knows how long I would have stayed there. This was a mistake I knew I wouldn't allow myself to make again. If I ever felt complacent again, I would be aware of it as a tendency next time and prevent it from taking hold at all costs, because all it would end up doing would be to hold me back from being somebody great.

TAKING CONTROL OF MY OWN LIFE

•

"WHETHER YOU THINK YOU CAN OR WHETHER YOU THINK YOU CAN'T—YOU'RE RIGHT."

—HENRY FORD

•

When I started pursuing my dreams, there were a lot more reasons for me to stop working toward them than there were to follow through. You see, videos and storytelling were always something I loved to do. Growing up with my brothers, whenever my parents would leave the house, we would secretly borrow the video camera to record ourselves wrestling in our underwear in the living room with the floor covered with pillows and blankets. We didn't think far enough ahead to realize that our parents would find the tapes, since we had left them in the cameras, but there was a magic behind storytelling in front of a camera that I fell in love with.

And as we got older, that love of wrestling evolved into recording our wrestling matches in the park with our friends. We each had different characters we played, and little kids from all over the park would stand around the small gated tire swing area to watch us hit each other with steel chairs, slam each other through doors, and trash talk each other before every match. For years to come, our wrestling characters evolved, as did the production and quality of what we were creating. Eventually I got more involved in the storytelling part of it all, writing storylines, creating dramatic angles for different wrestlers' involvement, and even meeting with people months in advance to plan things out for the next summer.

At some point, though, we began to realize that we were indeed getting older and that our park wrestling days were coming to a close simply because we had other priorities in our lives. I was in college then, taking a video class with my older brother. The final project for the class was to record a semi-long form video, so we decided to record a pilot for a web series we wanted to create. Our professor had told us that the final projects would be shown in the college theater on the big screen so we could invite our friends to check it out.

My brother and I told everyone about it, so two cars full of people drove up to our school to watch the debut of our comedy web series. The only issue was that they never played it that night, leaving all of our friends dumbfounded and disappointed. I felt confused and embarrassed, so I approached the professor at the end of class and asked why she had not showed it, only to be told, "It was pretty bad, but you can watch it now if you want." The theater was empty by then, and my hope of creating a web series was crushed.

The crushed feelings were short-lived, however, because soon enough my friends and I got back into creating skits for YouTube. I started to feel like this was something I could really do, something I could spend the rest of my life doing,, because it was so much fun to bring stories to life like that. We continued making skits until our comedy dreams had come to the same fate as our wrestling: everyone had other priorities in their lives.

I started to question if this was the right path for me. It seemed nearly impossible for me to maintain a creative effort that I enjoyed and to find people who were just as passionate as I was. That's when I met a young woman whose ambition matched mine on every level. She wanted to create a comedy show on YouTube where she would dress up in costumes, play different characters, and interview people about the craziest things. Now this was something I was fully on board with; I had the freedom to create scripts and to produce videos, while working with someone who understood my dream.

Once again, though, the long path forward came to a screeching halt when she could no longer make videos because her job wouldn't allow it. I felt like I had been chasing the dream of being a creator for years and had never quite found the right path for myself. I still wanted to pursue making films, but I just didn't know how to go about it. I realized the best path for me was probably to work on video projects for companies and people who needed it. Through a mutual friend, I was set up with a project where I would record a commercial as a freelance gig in Manhattan. Unfortunately, as I will explain later, things worked out very badly for me and made me seriously question my desire to pursue film. I began thinking of all that had gone wrong that day. Was this the right path for me? Why was I so certain I could do this when every single time I'd tried, it had never worked out for me?

I thought back to that life-changing day in college and remembered: my purpose in life is to experience it, and the reason I should go on living is to share it with others.

That was the day I began making videos for my channel *The Josh Speaks*.

I was enjoying it. I was enjoying making videos about my thoughts on and experiences of things for the simple purpose of sharing them with others. That's when I realized I had finally figured it out. All this time I had been trying to define myself by someone else's standard. For the majority of my life it was my parents, then became my first boss, and then my friends and eventually strangers I wanted to work with. But now I was defining myself by my own standard; I was doing what I wanted to do and what made me happy.

Looking back, I've been making videos for years now covering hundreds of topics from developing friendships, starting conversations, and feeling like you're good enough to asking out your crush, managing school stress, and more. I've spoken to thousands of people along the way online, in schools, and in person with all kinds of life stories and struggles—but the one thing I've learned from my own experiences and from what I've heard is that each and every single person has exactly what they need to embrace the awkward and be somebody great. I didn't realize this at first, I didn't even think it was possible; it wasn't until I developed skills and confidence that I understood what purpose really is.

Not everyone has it all magically figured out. In fact, probably no one does. Life is a journey, and no one has the map. But a meaningful experience in life begins by simply taking steps in the right direction.

That is exactly what I want to help you come to realize through this book: that YOU can be somebody great— that building confidence and finding purpose take some small steps, but together, we *can* get there.

CHAPTER 1

Practicing Mindfulness

"YOUR ENTIRE LIFE ONLY HAPPENS IN
THIS MOMENT. THE PRESENT MOMENT
IS LIFE ITSELF. YET PEOPLE LIVE AS IF
THE OPPOSITE WERE TRUE AND TREAT
THE PRESENT MOMENT AS A STEPPING
STONE TO THE NEXT MOMENT–A MEANS
TO AN END." –ECKHART TOLLE

HOW TO BE IN THE HERE AND NOW

When you wake up in the morning and start your day, how much thought do you put into the idea of being awake? I'd imagine it isn't a lot, considering there are so many other things to do, like getting ready for school, preparing your lunch for work, or even just picking up your phone to dive into any notifications that may have come in after you lay down to go to sleep. For the most part, we're always ready to jump into the next moment ahead of us, ready to do something else even when we are in the process of doing something in that moment.

Have you ever brushed your teeth and thought about what clothes you were going to wear? Have you ever gotten on a bus or a train and thought about what you were going to do when you finished your classes for the day? Sometimes it feels so natural to do this, to just allow our minds to drift off into things we want to do. There are even times our minds drift backward and start to remind us of things that have happened, both good and bad. Maybe the night before you got into an argument with your parents, or you saw a post online by a friend that made you feel a little jealous; maybe you just feel trapped in your day-to-day cycle, and the idea of changing it seems completely out of your hands.

While the thoughts we experience can vary from time to time, it seems pretty consistent that we aren't really being in the here and the now. We're letting our mind jump forward into our future or we're delving into our pasts—we're anywhere but here. If this is such a normal thing that everyone does, what's the problem then? And if there is a problem, what can we do to resolve it?

First, let's take a few minutes to dive deep into this moment right now. As you read this book, I want you to step outside of yourself for a bit and observe whatever sensations you may be feeling as we walk through them. To start, think about how you're positioned. Are you sitting down on a comfortable couch or chair, are you standing on a bus or a train or are you lying in bed with a pillow behind your neck? However you're reading it, that simple sense of awareness you experienced for a brief moment about where you are is being in the here and the now. It can get even deeper than that if you're willing to continue with me.

As you continue to read I want you to focus now on your breath. Feel the air enter your lungs as you breathe in, hold that breath for just a second or two, and then exhale to let the air escape. Inhale one more time, feel the oxygen enter to a point where your lungs are full and whole, and then exhale again. While you breathe, try to imagine the air as something you can see entering your body, something you are bringing into it by your own sheer will. It's easy for us to forget how important breathing is, usually because it becomes so automatic to us and we just accept it as a part of life. But when we take a moment to be fully aware of it, we stop focusing so much on ideas of the past and the future. We take full control of the present moment that exists in the here and the now.

When you are conscious and aware of a specific moment in the present, you are practicing mindfulness. Mindfulness can seem like an abstract concept or can even come off as a buzzword to you, but there is a lot of power behind it. Being mindful can help you respond to all kinds of situations like not feeling good enough measured by someone else's standards, dealing with hurtful words from someone you care about, or worrying about a test you're taking later in the day.

When we think about mindfulness, we tend to imagine practicing it in a context that exists entirely on its own, outside of the real world that we live in. However, let's walk through each of those examples and see how we can use mindfulness to manage the emotions and feelings we have during those situations. Imagine you have a crush on someone that you've liked for a while. You're completely captivated by the way they look, they way they talk, and every other quality you've gotten to know about them. There may even be times where you find your mind drifting off into fantasy scenarios where you two are dating or how you would ask them out if you had the opportunity to do so. These type of thoughts can make you feel happy, but they don't have a chance of coming to be unless you do something about it.

When the time finally does come for you to approach the person and talk to them, you mess it all up. You don't say the right kind of words, your body language is awkward and nervous, and they tell you they don't have romantic feelings and just see you as nothing more than a friend. Moments like these can feel soul-crushing, it can take all the expectations you've had and flip them upside down, leaving you feeling like there's something wrong with you, like you're not good enough to date them, or that happiness is just not possible for you now.

It's moments like these where mindfulness training can help us work toward feeling whole again. Otherwise, we will allow ourselves to naturally fall into the cycle of thinking of those painful events and reliving all the things we could have done differently, despite not having the ability to change the past at all. What we can do instead is close our eyes and focus deeply on our breathing once again. Rejection and heartbreak are part of the past, not the present. And as we bring ourselves into the present, the past can stay where it is. If you find your mind wandering back to those thoughts and feelings, understand that they exist and they have their reality, but they don't need to be here right now with us. Think of these thoughts as waves of water coming onto a beach and wetting the sand. As the thought comes in, you may feel like it's here to stay, like it's a part of your present existence and there's nothing you can do about it. But once you recognize you are thinking it, center yourself once again and come back to the present. Come back to the breath, and let the waves gently retreat back into the ocean. Or maybe your mind isn't centered around your mistakes, perhaps your mind is focusing on how you can recover from your mistakes and what needs to be done to fix the situation. These thoughts too can also be put on hold for now, the key is to remain here in the present because it's in the present where your feelings exist. There will be a time to work on changing things, but without a clear mind your decisions will be driven by your anxiety and fears.

Where you stand, as you feel your body breathing in, everything in this moment is OK. You are not being rejected, you are not trying to recover from a mistake, you are simply existing as you are, right here and right now. There is no other time that exists but this moment, and in this moment, you are whole. You can become grounded in the idea that this is where you stand, you can feel your feet planted on the ground, you can feel your legs keeping you there, and you can feel that *you* are what exists, not others' image of you.

Practicing meditation can be difficult, but it is even more difficult at times to apply it to real-world scenarios. When you are especially hurt, your instinct might be to escape the pain rather than absorb it and transform it. Regardless of what you choose to do, however, you should always know that you have the strength to get through it as you continue to breathe, and this is not something anyone can ever take away from you.

Let this bring you peace over time—recognize that the choices and words of someone else are how they felt at the time, and that the feelings they carried don't have to come with you—you can choose to let them go.

Let's also imagine that you're preparing for a big exam in school, the kind of exam that can make or break your final grade for the class. You've spent a great deal of time studying for this test, but you still feel nervous about taking it because you don't know what to expect. The idea of how the experience may feel continues to play in your head in a loop, and you feel helpless to think otherwise.

Before your test, you can practice mindfulness to help you resolve the stress that thoughts of the future moment may be causing, and all it requires you to do is to return to the here and the now. In this very moment, you are not taking your exam and you are not studying for it. You are existing in the very present, where there is no test to complete but rather a test to let go of. The reason why you may be worrying about it is because the test starts to take shape in place of who you are. You see your worth as how well you will perform on the test, and because of this, you lose sight of your identity, your body, and your breath.

Sometimes when people are studying for a test, they forget to eat, they lose out on sleep, and they let it affect all the other aspects of their life. The test becomes your present moment, and it's only by practicing mindfulness that you can see that you are not your exam. All you are is someone who exists right here. You have a greater purpose. If you close your eyes and focus once again on your breath, you'll start to see that what's to come is not what is; all you can control is what you have access to in this moment.

The next challenge is to take your exam and then to wait for your grade to see how you did. This can also create a sense of anxiety and can lead you back into projections of the future. You hope you did well but worry that you got questions wrong or should have chosen a different answer for a few of the questions. It's in these moments that it serves you best to let go—you cannot know the outcome of the test until it has been graded, and thinking about the grade will not make it come about any faster. So what can you do while you wait? You can practice mindfulness.

Whenever you feel like your mind is leading you to worry about your grade, remember that no matter what may happen, you will still live past it. It can be easy to feel like moments like these can totally ruin our lives, but as long as we can return to our breath, as long as we are alive, and as long as we possess the ability to keep moving forward, nothing can prevent us from doing so. Putting the mindfulness practices we learned earlier can help us return to a place of calm and can allow us to step outside of our worrying for a moment in time.

Being in the here and the now is a matter of accepting what is real, and accepting what is real can feel counterintuitive to what our brains may be telling us sometimes. But with practice, we can work on implementing mindfulness training into different aspects of our lives, not just the ones where we feel awkward, powerless, or hurt. Mindfulness should be practiced when we are happy as well because it can allow us to fully experience the joy of the moment and take all of it in while it's happening.

LIVING A MINDFUL LIFE PATH

•

"IF YOU LOOK DEEPLY INTO THE PALM OF YOUR HAND, YOU WILL SEE YOUR PARENTS AND ALL GENERATIONS OF YOUR ANCESTORS. ALL OF THEM ARE ALIVE IN THIS MOMENT. EACH IS PRESENT IN YOUR BODY. YOU ARE THE CONTINUATION OF EACH OF THESE PEOPLE."

–THICH NHAT HANH

•

Walking a path of mindfulness is a lifelong process that can be started as soon as right now. Nothing is required to start being mindful; there are no degrees you have to obtain, and there is no place in life you have to get to. Where you are, as you are, is all you need to start experiencing the world in the present moment. For some people that moment of realization can come as a spark, a change that just takes over your mood and sense of being and propels you to start noticing things you've never noticed before.

My own journey into mindfulness started when I was in college. Looking back, I wish I had prepared earlier, I wish I'd had someone to propel me in a direction that would not only match my personality and interests but would also align with my skill set and what I was good at overall. I was sad because I had let myself down, but I felt even worse because I had let my parents down. They were so proud of me for going to college, and even though I knew that the direction of computer engineering wasn't the right one for me, I just couldn't bring myself to tell them I wanted to switch. If only I had realized in the very beginning that my life path could only be determined by myself, I would have made my decision more critically. None of my growth afterwards would have happened, though, had I not had my breakthrough and had I not found my reason for existence.

To some people the whole idea of finding yourself may sound like a strange concept, maybe even a cheesy one, but it's so important to stop and reflect on the person we want to be by taking a moment to tap into who we are right now.

Living a mindful path is possible for you as long as you're open to slowing things down, taking a breather, and being in the moment. As I passed through college and then going forward, I felt more awake than ever. Whenever I would walk to class. I would really see things as they happened, not just on the surface, instead observing them in a way where I felt the interconnectivity of myself and the world around me. In one particular area of my school campus, there was a pathway through the woods that you could walk through as a shortcut; on one side of the road was a tall stone that pointed upwards, seeming to symbolize rising up from the ground and reaching for the sky. On the other side of the road was a dead tree, fallen and rotten, an icon of death and decay, the end of all things. Every time I walked in between these two symbolic trees, I felt a renewed sense of energy and the realization that I could reach as far as I wanted. We are either growing, or we are dying. We can choose. Even though we have a limited time on earth, we can all make the most of the time we have been given.

All of this was simply the start of my mindful path. With each passing year, I learned more and more about myself, my connection to the world, and how I played a role in all of it. I started to realize that my body was the only one I had and that I needed to treat it right, or else I wouldn't have a vessel to live in to continue forward. This led me onto the path of exercise; I felt so connected to exercising because I knew that by training I was doing the one thing that no one else could do for me. While education was mandatory, only I could make myself healthy and strong with exercise—and it was up to me to be successful at it. For a lot of people, fitness is seen as something we do because we aspire to look better or gain muscles. We rarely see it as a way of loving our body, taking care of it, and shaping it so we can be ready to be to tackle any challenges that come our way.

When we exercise, we aim to take care of ourselves. As I exercised more and more, experiencing my new strength led me to ask myself how much more I was capable of doing. My goal had been to work toward helping other people. Now that I was more equipped to tackle any physical challenges, I had to put that into play. It wasn't until much later on, however, that I also discovered a second aspect to nurturing your body— maintaining good health. Growing up, I had never had a single desire to drink alcohol, smoke marijuana, or try cigarettes. The idea of taking anything that might alter my state of mind just wasn't enticing enough for me. I felt like being in the moment was enough for me to feel that same sense of high, and I never wanted to become dependent on anything to get me there.

For years I had eaten pretty poorly, not really thinking about my food choices or where my food had come from. I had aspired to be mindful but was still neglecting a huge part of my day-to-day life. This is the journey of a mindful path—as you continue learning and growing, you begin to incorporate more and more changes as you work toward being your best self. My girlfriend at the time (now my wife) was a vegetarian and was pretty turned off by the things I would regularly eat. I was a heavy consumer of meat, eggs, and pizza. I had always eaten food that was fast, fried, or processed without a second thought as to how it was affecting me. Part of it was the culture I had grown up around and the normalization of bad habits.

When I began to think about where my food came from, there was a level of awareness that had seemed hidden to me before. I had become so used to cultural food norms that I never stopped to realize the harm that came with my choices. That is why in the process of being mindful, it's important to trace back what comes with our food, and to think about how it was made and the implications of those actions. For example, when we think of eating a hamburger, we see the food as simply a piece of meat that is cooked, seasoned, and eaten.

However, before the meat was just meat, it was part of a cow that was born with feelings and the ability to suffer like you and me. No living being wants to die, or would choose to die if the alternative was to live freely. But when we eat, we ignore this truth because it may make us hesitate in eating the hamburger.

Some people will justify the means and say it is just the way things are, but much like with anything, we have the ability to choose to be mindful and act. We can choose to reduce harm and suffering, but that means being mindful of where our food comes from. This process of backtracking is essential if we want to be mindful and aspire to reach our highest potential, whether it's reconsidering buying clothing that was made by slave labor, food that resulted in the unnecessary suffering of animals, or an argument we got into with someone we care about.

If we wish to truly walk a mindful path in life, we need to start with each and every step we take and ask ourselves: am I walking in a way brings kindness to those around me? This will make you a model for others who are struggling—leading by example—and will help you to become your best self.

DAILY MINDFULNESS EXERCISES

I started to discover more and more mindfulness techniques when I watched the documentary *Samsara*. In one of the opening scenes, there are several Buddhist monks creating an elaborate work of art made of sand on a canvas. To make these designs, it requires several people and a meticulous sense of design to craft the patterns, curves, lines, and shapes for it. Each work of art can take several hours to create, producing a beautiful masterpiece in the end.

At the end of the documentary *Samsara*, something happened that made me realize the broader message that the movie was trying to portray. Once the Buddhist monks completed the artwork, they stood around and marveled in the glory of their hard work; and then they brushed it all away with brooms, instantly destroying (or as I would later discover, changing) the sand art and turning it back into what it had been originally, a canvas with unlimited possibilities.

Even after devoting all that time and energy into making the sand art, they were able to appreciate it just for a moment and then to let it go. It's not easy to let go of something you worked hard to create, especially if you feel like you've invested a lot of time and energy into it. Sometimes we think it defines who we are or what our purpose is.

There was a lesson to be learned there, something I could take away with me. It was the knowledge that even though I was not a Buddhist monk but just a regular guy, I could move through life with the assertiveness to be in the moment—to experience all that it could bring me—until it was time to let it go and move on to the next one.

If you're taking an exam for school, that moment may be letting go of the anxiety you feel when the test is over and you're worrying about what grade you got, or how you could have answered a question better. If you're thinking about asking someone out, that moment might be working up the courage to ask and encountering your fear of the potential rejection that may come with it. Being able to accept that, whatever happens doesn't define you will allow you to embrace however it turns out.

And the amazing thing is, there are no limitations to what this mindset can be applied to—from managing friendship drama to getting a job you're happy with. Where most people tend to struggle is focusing on being present, no longer worrying about what was or what will be, and the reason for that is because we don't always have the tools to help us practice.

However, what I've come to learn is that you can take any activity and use it as a reminder to be in the here and the now. When I was in college, I used my walks to class as a time to focus on my feet as they touched the ground, and whenever I did that, I wasn't worried about anything other than living in that experience. Some Buddhist monks carry around tiny little pebbles in their pockets so that whenever they stick their hands in there and feel them, they can realign their mindset to what is happening then and there. The feeling of the small pebble between their fingers, the hard, rough consistency of it, the light and almost airy weight, and any other factor that may come to their minds serve as reminders when they do this.

Even tasks in your day-to-day life can be mindfulness reminders if you allow them to be. The next time you have to do chores around the house, let's say when it's your job to wash the dishes, try to take in every element that you can: the warm water against your hands, the feeling of the sponge as it rubs against the plate, the sound of the water hitting the dishes, even the smell of the soap. What you'll begin to see is that even the most dull and boring moments can be transformed into mindfulness practices.

You can also practice with everyday sounds, like the bell ringing for you to go to the next class, or the doors opening and closing on the subway as you get on. Feel the experience of that moment, breathe, and let your mind enjoy it. In some cases this won't be easy, especially if you find yourself with other people, or if you're really focused on an activity at hand and the last thing you want is an interruption. What it comes down to is not looking at mindfulness as a distraction from life but as an opportunity to truly be in it.

So, that's what I want you to try. Meditation doesn't have to be sitting on the floor with your legs crossed, trying to be one with nature—it's simply being aware of where you are, and in that awareness, you'll start to see that level of interbeing (a term coined by Thich Nhat Hanh) in everything around you. All of life exists with you, and everything is sharing that experience as well. A simple solution might also be to find a meditation app that will send off the sound of a bell every so often to help bring you back to the now. And what are you supposed to do if your friends are with you, trying to get your attention or just curious as to why you seemed so tuned into whatever you're doing? Well, invite them to join you!

Some of the most rewarding experiences happen when you practice meditation and mindfulness with others. The energy of that experience can be even stronger for you if you know that others are tapping into the joy of being alive in the present moment. Forming a meditation group can be super empowering because it gives you and your friends the ability to connect on a deeper level, most likely on a much more peaceful level than you're used to with them.

Either way, try to find a way that works for you; it can be for a few seconds a day or a few minutes a week. Let your mindfulness journey be your own—you can't screw it up, and you can't fail at it. See it as something safe; it's something to turn to when everyone or everything else in the world feels like they're at odds with you. Because at the end of the day, no matter how someone may come down on you for it, you can only approach it from this moment, not any other. And the closer connected you are with this moment, the easier it will be to move through life.

CHAPTER SUMMARY + EXERCISES

In this chapter we talked about the importance of mindfulness in learning to accept the conditions of the world around you so you don't get pulled into a world of thought that controls you. While it may seem like being present is an obvious state to be in, our minds are tricky things, and if left to their own devices, they will keep us from ever feeling like where we are in this moment is good enough.

Learning to be mindful was a journey for me, one that I only allowed myself to be open to once I was able to let go of where I felt I "should" be. Instead I accepted where I was. It didn't mean giving up or losing clarity and direction in my life—it meant recognizing the step in which I stood, rather than looking back at the steps I had already taken or the steps that were yet to come.

What I want you to start working on is incorporating small mindfulness practices into your daily routine. Everything is small steps, so there's no need to expect that the following tasks will be easy to do day after day. The most important step here is to try your best.

MORNING

When you first wake up, it might feel natural to reach over and check your phone to see what time it is or if you have any notifications that require your immediate attention.

Before you launch into checking anything, sit upright in your bed and stick your arms out way above your head and stretch your body.

Then, bring your arms out to your side and take a deep breath in. As you bring your arms back down to your sides, stretch your spine straight up, and then allow yourself to stand up and start your day.

Okay, now you can run and check your phone.

Chances are your morning meal is the only meal when you're going to have a moment of peace and quiet (if you have the time to eat breakfast; if not, try to make the time). If your routine already includes you checking your phone, watching TV, or multitasking while you're eating, take three minutes in the very beginning to focus on the experience of eating.

Be present for each and every bite, sit in silence, and just enjoy the taste of the food. Smell it as you raise it to your mouth, and focus on the depth of where the food came from, how it was prepared, and what went into the process of making it.

SCHOOL DAY/WORK DAY

During the day, our minds are running all over the place trying to think about what our next task is. We never have a moment to slow things down and just accept where we are and who we are in the present.

It can be difficult to suddenly realize that your mind is not in the present, so one of many ways to allow yourself to return to "the now" is to use markers to help you get there. One marker I would use in college was doorways. Whenever I would walk into or out of a room and pass through the doorway, I would take a breath and come back to the now. It's sort of like thinking about how you're blinking; when your mind connects to the idea that you are doing it, you suddenly become aware of each blink and can't *not* think about it.

Another technique you can try is carrying an object in your pocket so when you notice that it's there, you will be reminded to take your mindful moment. Buddhists practice this by carrying small pebbles inside of their pockets, and whenever they stick their hands in their pockets and feel them, they remember to be in the here and now.

There are lots of different ways to do this. For you, it might be when you're walking through the hallway at school, when you first sit down at your desk to work, or even when you hear the sound of the bell at your school signaling you to go to the next class.

RETURNING HOME

After a long day, you might feel exhausted to the point where all you want to do is lie down in front of the TV or computer to zone out. And while that's totally fine to do, the moment before you sit down could present you with the opportunity to practice mindfulness.

Before you launch into any activity, take a seat on your couch, chair, or bed, and sit up with a straight back so you can take in a deep breath. Most likely you've been on the move all day long, so letting this moment be the buffer where you can slow down before launching into your next activity will help you re-calibrate your body.

You might be feeling anxious to jump into whatever you're going to do next, but try the breathing techniques for one minute. If you have the time, do it for three minutes. And then when you're ready, pick up your remote or open up your laptop and move into the rest of your day.

BEFORE BED

When it's time for you to head to sleep, there isn't anything left for you to do besides lie down and pass out. Practicing mindfulness as you lie down to sleep can not only help you fall asleep more easily but can also bring you into a calm state of being where you won't be overrun by thoughts all night long.

Start simply by lying down on your back or in a comfortable position with your eyes closed. As you begin to breathe, move your focus to the different parts of your body. Start with the air going into your lungs, and then shift your focus to your chest and upper body. Feel your body sink into the bed below you, and release any tightened muscles. Let yourself feel as if you are floating on a cloud or on the surface of water.

Let your mind move in thought to the other parts of your body, your arms, your legs, and eventually your body as a whole. It's normal for your mind to wander or for you to think about what you have to do the next day, but at least for now in the moments when you first lie down, your mind is there with you.

CHAPTER 2

Recovering from Failure

"IF YOU'RE NOT WILLING TO WORK
HARD, LET SOMEONE ELSE DO IT.
I'D RATHER BE WITH SOMEONE WHO
DOES A HORRIBLE JOB BUT GIVES
110 PERCENT THAN WITH SOMEONE
WHO DOES A GOOD JOB AND GIVES 60
PERCENT." –WILL SMITH

IDENTIFYING YOUR STRENGTHS AND WEAKNESSES

There's a quote from Mister Rogers that I always turn to whenever I feel like I'm not taking action to the best of my ability. What I've come to learn over the years is that all we can ever give to any situation is ourselves. We can never be what someone expects us to be; heck, we can't even always be what WE want to be. And that's why it's a wonderful feeling to know that the most we can ever offer is our honest selves. This is the quote I turn to:

> "Sometimes people are good, and they do just what they should. But the very same people who are good sometimes are the very same people who are bad sometimes. It's funny but it's true. It's the same isn't it, for me and you."

Learning what you're good at is way more than just identifying your skill set or your ability to succeed in a single area of your life. When we're young, we're taught to think in this one-pointed way, to just find a career that will offer stability, security, and safety. These three "S" words leave the great majority of people pursuing dreams and goals that they may not want, but which are in alignment with the people with whom they surround themselves. In high school, this can take the shape of taking certain extracurricular activities or picking a college that your parents want you to attend; in college, this may be choosing the major that you know will enable you to get a job, and in adult life this may be staying exactly where you are for fear of having to start all over again.

If instead we started thinking about what our strengths and weaknesses actually are early on in our lives, I believe we would be better able to get on the path of pursuing a life that is fulfilling and meaningful. When we think of our strengths and weaknesses, we often define them simply as what you're good and bad at doing. It's as clear cut as that; it's trying to figure out what you already are capable of and running with that. But just like Mister Rogers said, the very same people who are good sometimes are the very same people who are bad sometimes. Just because you're good at something doesn't mean you have everything you need to know about it figured out.

A surgeon who is excellent at his job may really have no talent at comforting patients before they go into operation, or a teacher who is incredibly educated on a subject may be horrible at sharing that knowledge in a way that a student can understand. Every path you take has multiple layers to it, which is why it's so important to not measure your strengths and weaknesses by what you already possess, but instead by what you are capable of learning and growing into.

If you're open to learning, then you have the willingness to recognize that you may not be perfect at something, and that there may be a thing or two that you can learn from others that may give you a tremendous advantage in life, all because you were open to listening. Normally, what we're looking for is for someone to confirm our way of thinking. If people tell us that we're doing things just right, then we won't have to worry about the tougher part of it all, the need for growth. In fact, if your teacher gave you an A on every exam, would you ever feel like you needed to study?

It's in the hardships, the failures, and the setbacks that we have no choice but to confront the situation in front of us and say, "What could I do differently here?" Building up your strengths then becomes a lifelong process of not knowing what the right next step is but aiming for it anyway. And far more often than not, what you tend to discover is that your greatest strengths are in areas where you never would have expected them to be.

So if you're someone who's awkward around others and you don't really feel like there's one thing in particular that you're good at, find something you *want* to be good at, and look at all the activities that surround it. Let's say, for example, you want to be someone who other people look up to—someone who is really smart, charming, funny, and popular. All of these things may seem like your biggest weaknesses if you're not getting good grades, feel socially awkward around others, and get nervous when you talk to people. A pretty normal response might be to just envy the people who are where you want to be, to look at them and think that they have it all figured out, that they are living your dream, and you're not moving through life at your full potential.

And while sometimes that may feel like the right way to think about it, it's not taking in the full story. Because everyone *has* a story, and knowing more about someone's story helps you piece together more and more how they got to where they want to be. First, try to observe them when they are around other people. Do they typically start conversations? How do they act when someone jokes around with them? How much focus do you see them dedicate to performing at the level at which they're performing? Learning all this about someone else is a lot harder than just assuming they have it all figured out. But once we start to realize that every person gets to where they are by dedicating themselves to what they want, it should become more and more transparent that it's just as possible for us to do the same.

What if, for example, there's someone who is super attractive to the point where people are doing anything and everything for them? I know some of the first thoughts that would pop into my head are that they maybe are undeserving of the attention and care they're receiving, or that they are only getting those things because of their looks—that if they didn't look good no one would care about them. It's easy to feel that way when looks or attention are things you struggle with. That's why I would say to use the same techniques here, and ask yourself questions about how they got to where they want to be. Do they highlight their best physical qualities? Are they putting themselves into situations where they can get more attention or get noticed? Having that sense of awareness can help you better understand someone else, even if you don't intend on doing the same things they have done to get to the level where they are.

And that's another important thing to keep in mind: just because someone has a method for putting their strengths front and center doesn't mean that you have to follow the same exact path. More often than not, the finish line that we're all looking to cross leads to many different ways of celebrating. So while you may aspire to have the same treatment or opportunities as someone else, it will always take a different shape for you when you get there. How then should you go about finding what your natural strengths are compared to what you want to build and work on?

The first step is to look at how you treat and interact with the closest people around you. More often than not, that's a good indicator of what you excel in and also what you need to work on. When you think about those individuals, do you feel a sense of warmth, care, and respect toward them? Are you loving, accepting, and compassionate toward them even when they don't do what you want them to do? These are tough questions to ask, and even if you feel like the answer is no, it only shows that this may be the first area you want to work on and build into a strength. Because who you surround yourself with is vital to your own development; these will be the people who will try their best to keep you focused, to call you out when you may be acting out of line, and who will have your back when you feel like nothing is working out.

Building a strong network of people also means cutting ties with the people who are bringing you down. If there's someone in your life who tries to shame you for pursuing your goals—stop sharing your most passionate dreams with them. If there's someone who creates so many issues for you that you aren't allowed to really work on yourself—limit the time you spend with them, and set boundaries that you plan on sticking to. What you want to have are goal-oriented, passionate, and caring people around you when you journey into the unknown to learn something new.

And just as iron sharpens iron, those people will help you sharpen your strengths as you do the same for them. Where can you find these types of people though? Should your network be your family, your school friends, your religious group, or even people you meet online? What really matters most is what works for you—just don't be afraid to let some of them go if they no longer support you going forward.

Try to center your path of growth around the qualities you see in other people that you would want for yourself. If a person is strong, protective, and stands up for you, isn't that a strength you would also want to possess? If a person is witty and makes you feel like everything is cool, wouldn't that be an awesome quality to have? Try to take note of the good behaviors you see others exhibit so you can find your own ways of getting there too. We tend to focus more so on vanity behaviors like looks, outward skills, and anything else that you can easily show off to others, but deep down, the ones that are most needed are the strengths that drive human connection.

And you may be thinking that you just don't have it in you. You're too nervous of a person to make others feel comfortable—how can you possibly demonstrate that quality if you are struggling with it yourself? That's a totally fair feeling to have, but it doesn't mean the situation is closed shut. There will always be moments where you don't feel like you're capable of accomplishing what you want, but everything takes small steps. So if you can look at the behaviors you want to display and ask yourself what doing 1 percent of that behavior looks like, it might just make it all the more possible for you.

Another great deterrent that makes people quit trying to pursue what they want in life is the time it takes to get there. If complications along the way pop up and add just a little more distance to your journey, it may just seem easier to quit while you're ahead. That's exactly how I felt in college when I failed my first semester of classes. I was ready to give up only because I didn't know what I wanted to pursue, and encountering challenges when you don't know what you want makes the whole thing seem pointless. But if you want to get over the time barrier and you want to see beyond how long it's going to take you to "be perfect" at what you're aiming for, you need to know where your target is.

Part of developing your strengths is knowing what you struggle with and knowing how you want to be overall. Say for example that you want to be a more understanding person, but you've had way too many situations where you accept people back into your life only for them to hurt you again. You might find it easier to lock yourself up and shut people out as a defense mechanism to protect yourself. But if you look beyond that and see that what you truly want is for people to respect you, your time, your worth, and your feelings, then it's possible you can approach being understanding in a completely different way.

Perhaps instead of giving everyone the same level of influence on you that you gave them before, you set up healthy boundaries as to how much input they have in your life. That way you are allowing yourself to be understanding without making a black-and-white call on every person you talk to. Developing that foresight isn't easy, but as you inch toward what you want, as you identify the qualities in others that you admire, and as you are humble enough to know what you need to work on, you'll start to craft your best strengths to be at the forefront of every encounter you have.

HOW TO ASK FOR HELP

When you think of someone who needs help, does the idea of someone weak pop into your head? It's very common to feel that asking for help means admitting weakness—it says that there is something we aren't good at, that we don't understand, and that we aren't smart enough to figure out on our own. The stigma that asking for help is weakness has always been around, and it's usually accompanied by the thought that strong people figure things out on their own. If we stop and examine that idea and look at what is driving it, we will recognize that it's an emotional response driven by the need to feel loved, cared for, and included.

The vulnerability that comes with asking for help means accepting that there is a point where you don't have full control. It's hard to knowingly walk into a situation like that because our natural instincts try to keep us prepared and alert at all times. I encountered that idea firsthand in a conversation with one of my friends in college during the time when dating books and guides were becoming more widespread and popular. For me, I was always curious to challenge what I knew, and I found it even more intriguing when I came across something that opened up my mind to a new world of ideas.

I was walking with a friend when I told him about one of the dating books I had been reading, sharing my learning moments with him out loud and openly, without concern for anyone who might be listening in on our conversation. When I asked him if he had read any books on the topic before, his voice became quiet and he started to panic, looking to see if anyone around us was listening for his response. He then very timidly told me that he had, but didn't want anyone to know because he was afraid people would make fun of him for not knowing how to successfully talk to girls to begin with.

I was confused at first as to why he would be so scared of people finding out. What was the big deal with learning how to do something by reading about it from a book? But as I dug deeper into it, I realized that his fear wasn't about the act of reading to learn—it was about the expectation he thought others had of him to just figure it out on his own. He was scared to turn to a book for help because having to read a book meant he was incapable of succeeding without effort. This is something that gets repeated in multiple areas of our life; we're held to a standard often not even set by ourselves, yet we still cling to it just so we can fit in. Asking for help is not admitting defeat; on the contrary, I see it as the most honorable thing you can do, because it means you're willing to accept two very important things:

1. You don't have all the answers; and
2. You're not a bad person for not already knowing something.

Something you should learn early on is that no one has all the answers. No one you'll ever meet has it all figured out, and there's not one person on this planet who can say they are able to handle every situation they encounter with complete certainty about how it's going to work out. In theory, that sounds obvious—until we start to apply it to the real people around us whom we consider "perfect." For you, it might be your parents or relatives; you might feel like they have it all together because all throughout your life they have been the people you've turned to for advice or help. As hard as it is to accept, even they are moving through life trying to figure it all out. When you're fifteen years old, you won't know precisely how to handle life in the same way as when you're twenty-five, so what makes you think that when you're fifty-five, you'll know how to handle your life at sixty-five? We're all taking small steps forward—learning as we go—and this can be something we overlook when it comes to the people who take care of us. If we accept that they aren't perfect, then it means coming to grips with our own not being perfect as well.

Alternately, you may look at your friends or your classmates as people who have all the answers and who know exactly what to say to start relationships, do well in school, or plan out their future. Sure, sometimes people are good at playing the role of "having it together," but they too are learning as they go. This isn't to say that no one knows anything or that there is no certainty or structure in life that you can map out and predict—let's not get black-and-white about it. The truth, however, is probably found somewhere in the middle. Thinking the cool guy in school with the attractive girlfriend, the scholarship, and the career path of a millionaire got there because of his keen insight and abilities alone comes naturally to us. But skill, effort, and work play a major role in how we succeed. There's also the unspoken act of asking for help along the way.

Help comes in many different forms. Sometimes it's very practical and can be in the form of direct advice, like laying out a step-by-step process for how to do something. Other times it is more indirect and comes in the form of support, such as sitting and listening to someone vent about a bad test grade or a fight they had with a friend. For those who tend to succeed, a major factor in their development ends up being that they are surrounded by loving and supportive people who are willing to help them when they need it. For those who don't receive that kind of support, the burden is left for them to figure it out on their own—which can often be coupled with resentment toward others for not stepping in.

What do you do then, if you don't have anyone you can turn to for support and guidance? What if you're by yourself—with no one to direct you, listen, or teach you how to move forward in a way that will help you feel confident? You can do exactly what you're doing right now: reading a book about embracing your awkwardness. This is you actively seeking help, and it's definitely something I can get behind. You might feel a sense of uneasiness about reading a book on how to figure out life—those feelings of judgment from others may start to creep up again—but that's why it's important to remember the second point I mentioned ... you're not a bad person for not knowing.

There's plenty in life that I don't know, and there's a high chance that even when I *think* I understand it, I'll be wrong a large percentage of the time. Our minds are made to grow and adapt to new information. So if we keep challenging ourselves to grasp new concepts and ideas, we won't feel as much resistance as we will if we try to limit our world views. This is a common thing for a lot of people. It becomes easier sometimes to rest on the things you've already learned, simply because learning something new means challenging the comforts of your lifestyle. If you believe you're doing something the right way, you are more likely to think it's the world around you that's wrong, and that if people could only get their act together, then you wouldn't be so frustrated and keep running into the issues you do.

If you're trying to ask out a person that you like but they just don't seem to notice you, having a limited perspective might lead you to think there's something wrong with them—that they aren't quite getting the signals and meeting your expectations. In fact, you might even think something is wrong with *you*, but instead of seeking help to work on it, you may think the problem is irreparable and that the outcome is set in stone. Your mind is going to spend a lot of time and energy trying to keep you where you are, but it's important to try to see past that—to recognize that overcoming the discomfort of the unknown might seem frightening at first, but it will get easier as time goes on.

So how can you actually ask for help? Do you just tell someone that you have a problem and want to learn what they know? Well, some of the greatest teachers are people who have experienced similar situations. More often than not, speaking to someone older than you is a good place to start because chances are they've had their fair share of heartbreak, failure, indecisiveness, and unmotivated moments throughout their lives. In many cases, older people may seem out of touch or totally disconnected from where you are in your life, but human emotion is human emotion. Sharing your story with someone and asking for their honest and empathic feedback might be the best way for them to learn more about you, and for you to learn more about yourself.

Asking for help isn't just a method of resolving a problem, it can also be a way of shedding light on things that may not be obvious to you until you talk about them. Admitting you are having trouble, therefore, is an enlightening moment—one that no one can ever knock down unless you give them the power to do that to you. Starting that conversation with the words "I feel" will allow you to be honest and make real progress with yourself. And the great thing is, there's no shortage of things you can learn from someone else. Each and every person has their own life experience to share, which can give you multiple perspectives on how to approach a situation.

Normally, when it comes to asking your friends for help, it can be a good thing, but it might also be a bad thing. On the upside, here are people just like you with similar obstacles in their way. Their insights and advice may be more authentic since they know you a lot better than someone from outside your circle would. However, as a downside, they may not have enough experience around a subject to know what it looks like on the other side. Say for example, you're working on a paper for school that counts as a large part of your final grade, but for some reason you keep slacking off and not dedicating the time to writing that you should. If you ask a friend, they may be able to tell you what you should do, like taking a half hour each day to at least write *something* to get it started. But what they probably won't be able to tell you is how you're going to feel once you complete the paper and get back your grade for the class. That's an experience reserved for someone who has already completed that element of their life, and can therefore share their full story.

The world has a lot to teach us, and the best way to learn is to understand the stories of those who have come before us. The beauty of it all is that most people *want* to share what they know, because deep down there is a willingness in many to prevent others from making the same mistakes. Because of that, we can be grateful for those who take the time to help us. Let them know how appreciative you are of them for sharing their experiences, and in turn, they'll let you know how grateful they are to you for listening.

THE VALUE OF YOUR WORK VS. YOUR WORTH

•

"DON'T QUIT. NEVER GIVE UP TRYING TO BUILD THE WORLD YOU CAN SEE, EVEN IF OTHERS CAN'T SEE IT. LISTEN TO YOUR DRUM AND YOUR DRUM ONLY. IT'S THE ONE THAT MAKES THE SWEETEST SOUND."

–SIMON SINEK

•

When we think about our place in the world, we generally look at where we are in relation to the people around us. We consider what the people in our age group have accomplished so far, and if we are more or less in line with what is expected of us. And while from a very basic perspective, this could be a good indicator of general growth, it also is the number one reason why people don't pursue their dreams or accomplish the things they truly want. **If we only look at what we can achieve in relation to what others have achieved, then no new standard will ever be created, and we won't always be waiting for someone else to set it for us.**

Of course, it's not necessarily our fault that we think like this. Many of us model our behaviors on the people we directly perceive—our parents, our teachers, and especially our friends. So much of our time is spent comparing ourselves to others, oftentimes to the point where we see everyone else as successful and ourselves as imitators, pretending we know what our next step is. This is why it is common to seek the quickest, easiest, and shortest path to happiness. The sooner we get to what we think "happy" is, the sooner we can stop questioning where we are, who we are, and why we are.

You probably know someone who has taken the quickest path to stability. Maybe they took the first job that came their way and decided that the pay is good enough (and the conditions aren't bad enough) for them to consider working somewhere else. Or maybe you know someone who immediately got into a relationship, just so they wouldn't be alone anymore. Having someone they can shift their everyday focus onto makes it easier for them not to think about *their own* capabilities and struggles. The quickest path always seems attractive, because it's the fastest way for us to prove that we can make something out of ourselves. When our parents see that, when our friends see that, and when the world sees that, they'll all think that we have value—and that value is driven solely by the assumption that we are useful somewhere.

What often gets coupled together are the ideas of choosing something quick and choosing something simple. Maintaining a simple life, however, doesn't mean you're settling for just anything that comes along. Ironically, living a simple life is slightly complex, if you think about what it takes to let go of our preconditioned ideas of what we need to be happy. Especially when it comes to work, **we don't have to aim high as much as aim straight toward what we want**. If we can see a future for ourselves, then we're making the decision to grow with what we're doing. However, if we only see our goals as something we are entitled to, instead of something we actually want (which makes it more meaningful), then we'll keep aiming up—only to have things fall back down on us at some point.

Where we choose to apply ourselves, therefore, matters so much. It matters not just because our time is limited and valuable, but because we have a choice where we place our talents and our ability to do meaningful things in this world. Not everyone sees their own potential, but it's there, so people choose the easy road without even knowing how far they can possibly go. There's a value to the work you do that only you can define. Even if you're working under someone else's goals, toward someone else's vision, and following someone else's lead, you are in the driver's seat and determine how much you can give.

At my first official job after college, it was easy for me to quickly learn the things I had to do. I worked as an email marketing specialist creating email campaigns to place technology products into college bookstores for sale. My bosses had an idea of what I would work on, but for the most part I had the free rein to design, be creative, and think outside of the box in how I marketed to those buyers. It was amazing at first, because I had found something in my life where I fulfilled a purpose. I was helping the world turn, and with each day the routine became ingrained in my life to the point where

I stopped thinking about doing it. The creative process became more and more systematic until, without even realizing it, I had moved into autopilot mode.

When you're on autopilot, you start to function in a way where you are completely blind to the fact that your fulfillment no longer comes from how you apply yourself during the day. Instead of waking up and living for what you do, you look forward to life *around* what you do. The few hours pursuing your hobby after work, the two-day weekends after a long five-day workweek. Somehow, without even consciously realizing it, you make the trade of happiness for contentment and it totally flies over your head.

I remained at my first job for four years, and my tasks changed with time—I took on a little more responsibility as well—but overall, I was waiting for my workday to end so that I could move on to doing something I enjoyed. I kept telling my other coworkers that I would one day leave, but for some reason, I could never bring myself to do it. The idea of starting somewhere new, and the effort and time it would take to apply for new jobs, attend interviews, and worry about bringing home a certain level of income was a world I didn't want to enter. It wasn't until my boss called me and another coworker into the office one day to tell us that they were letting us go and outsourcing our jobs to another country that it finally hit me.

Somehow my autopilot had been turned off, and I felt a world of opportunity was opened for me once again. I still would have to spend the time applying to new jobs, traveling for interviews, and worrying about money, but ... now that it was a reality for me, I felt energized to go out there and try once more. I was willing to try and find a way to give my all to my work so I could feel fulfilled just like I had felt the first time. One of my biggest fears, however, was that I would eventually fall into the same cycle. Why is it so easy to fall into autopilot? Why can't we just love what we do and be happy every day doing it?

The answer, of course, is a lot simpler than we think it is. Most of us approach a job or a task focusing on the work we will have to do: we measure up how much time it would take for us to do it, we want to know what kind of thanks or recognition we'll get for taking on the role, or we simply want something to occupy our time. It isn't until we start to value our *worth* instead of our work that we truly love what we do, and even start to *live* for what we do.

For me, this was the start of my channel *The Josh Speaks*, which has become my life's purpose and something I want to do until the day I die. This wasn't the case in the beginning. In fact, I was just making videos for fun as a hobby, with no direction other than making a little bit of extra money on the side. I had tried several times to build YouTube channels in the past with my friends, but no one cared enough to stick it out on the projects, and eventually they would slow down until we just stopped completely. Afterwards, as I mentioned before, I tried my hand at freelance video work and took on a small gig recording a short commercial for a little league basketball team in uptown Manhattan, New York, approximately an hour and a half from where I lived at the time.

I woke up early on the morning that I was going to record, prepared all of my camera equipment, and headed off to the big city—only to find out that on that day, the trains were not functioning as they normally did. On the weekends, the train system would run local rather than express trains (which is something I had accounted for), but certain trains were not running at all, which made traveling to the city an extra special adventure for me that day. I kept looking at my watch as the time drew closer and closer to our meeting time, ever-hopeful that

I would get there just in the nick of time to fulfill my promise of recording the commercial. But that wasn't how things worked out for me. Instead, I arrived thirty minutes into the forty-five-minute session, covered in sweat because I had run all the way from the train stop, and was overwhelmed with disappointment when the instructor told me that I had shown up too late and they no longer wanted to work with me.

I felt totally distraught. Here I was, finally pursuing my passion and trying to make money from it, and I had messed up my very first time doing it. Maybe it was time for me to throw in the towel and stop with film altogether. Maybe I should have just stuck to what I learned in college and stayed at my marketing job doing things the safe way—the way that school had prepared me for. Maybe I should have, but it was not at all what I wanted. What I wanted was to keep trying, simply because this was what I loved, and if I couldn't make it work doing commercials for companies, maybe there was another way. It was 9 a.m. on that life-changing Saturday morning when I decided to walk to the nearest public park, set up my camera and tripod, and record a video about failure.

I didn't know what I was going to say, but I just felt like I needed to get my thoughts out of my head, and talking to the camera was the best way for me to do it. I made my short three-minute video, starting it off with the words that would become iconic of my YouTube videos for years to come—"Heya playas"—and from that point on, I knew I had discovered something I wanted to do for the rest of my life. Somehow, I knew this was it, even though I didn't have a plan or a strategy to make it something sustainable, I simply knew that this was where my worth would shine.

Over the next few years, I continued to grow my channel in a direction that has not only helped shape my lifestyle but also how I interact with others. The reason why it's so important to understand your work vs. your worth is because when you learn to apply your worth to what you do, you'll start to live it in every aspect of your life. With *The Josh Speaks*, my goal is to help anyone who watches learn how to be their best self, and that can only happen if I am making that same effort every day. When I think about making videos, interacting with viewers, and taking on new time-consuming tasks to grow my channel, there isn't a moment when I see it fall out of line with my values.

The beauty here is that you don't always have to strive to be your own boss or to take your ideas to the highest limits that they can go, you simply have to love what you do so much that how you apply yourself is a representation of who you are. And that's something you can do working for a big company, working as a freelancer, or doing just about anything. If you start to change your perception—to see the world as a place where your worth has value, with the potential to use that value for something meaningful—then when instances of failure spring up (and they always will), you'll know that you can work through them. No matter *where* you apply your skills, the fulfillment in applying those skills will give you worth, and remain with you each and every day.

CHAPTER SUMMARY + EXERCISES

In this chapter we talked about discovering what makes you special and getting over the idea that you need to be perfect for who you are to be acceptable. All it takes sometimes is one tiny negative experience to throw us off course and to make us start challenging our own accomplishments and abilities. We have the opportunity, however, to see those negative experiences either as acts of war or acts of clarity—whichever we choose will become our reality.

It's not easy, it might never be. But you don't ever have to go it alone. There are always helpers, people who are kind, caring, and loving. It may take time to seek them out, but they do exist. And that's why asking for help is a winning strategy. It shows you who you can turn to for help, and it gives you a window into how to be there for someone else.

Failure doesn't have to define you. That's why I want you to work on a few different activities that will help you to feel more comfortable turning to others for help and to recognize your own abilities to move past the hardships and tough roads you encounter. Some of these activities might seem a little off topic, but just like Mr. Miyagi wanted the Karate Kid to "wax on, wax off" with a cloth on a window so he could learn to block punches and kicks, so too will these activities help you realize that failure is only momentary.

MAKE THE FIRST "HELLO" OF THE DAY A SPECIAL ONE

Chances are that as you progress through your day, you'll encounter moments where you will have to speak to other people. We usually gloss over these simple interactions and never look at them as serious opportunities for us to build on our strengths, but that's something you can work on changing.

Use the chance to say hello to someone as a way to have a minor but significant human connection with them. That first person might be a family member, a bus driver, or a coworker—no matter who it is, see it as a chance for you to brighten someone else's day. Along with saying hello, ask them about something specific that you know about them or learn something new about them. Carry that person in your thoughts as you keep moving forward, and ask yourself what you can do or say the next time you see them to make them smile.

Part of moving past failure is remembering that we're all just people, people who want to feel accepted and cared for beyond what we can do. You deserve it and so do they, so make that first hello special.

OUTLINE ONE SMALL AND ACHIEVABLE GOAL THAT YOU CAN DO IN THE FIRST HALF OF YOUR DAY

Whenever we sit to write down our goals, we tend to incorporate lots of big lofty goals instead of small, actionable ones, which can make us lose sight of what is achievable right now. There's probably one or two things that you want to do but have put off for later simply because investing some time in it might not feel like *enough* time to make a difference.

You can change that, though, all you have to do is outline one small goal and stick to it. This could be anything from doing pushups in the morning, learning more about a potential hobby you want to pursue, or even catching up with an old friend who you haven't talked to in a long time.

Aim to do this small goal in the first half of your day. Something you'll start to realize is that by tackling something meaningful early on, the feeling of accomplishment will stay with you for the rest of the day.

POSE THREE QUESTIONS TO THREE DIFFERENT PEOPLE

Being vulnerable and asking for help can be difficult to do if you're battling with the idea of protecting yourself from looking weak in front of others. But normalizing the idea of learning from other people makes it easier and easier to turn to them for help.

Whenever you come across a task or topic that involves someone else, ask them about it, and really pay attention to what they have to say. We all carry different experiences, so even if someone has a limited view on a certain topic, hearing their view will help you expand your own perspective. Do this task with three different people every day so you can really make it a habit.

By engaging in this practice, you'll slowly start to train yourself to turn to others when you see opportunities to connect. And while there's nothing wrong with trying to figure things out on your own, it can make experiencing failure much harder to deal with when you haven't explored all your options for learning how to manage situations better.

SHARE SOMETHING POSITIVE

When times get tough, we may sometimes seek out things or share things that will reaffirm our negative emotions simply because it makes us feel better. The major problem with that is that when other people are in that same headspace, a bubble is created where the world looks like a worse place to live with every passing second.

Instead, rewrite the script and look for something positive to break up the negative monotony. If you recently failed a test, went through a bad breakup, can't get along with your family members, or any other situation that might be eating at you, look for something good happening in the world and share it for others to see.

This isn't a way to mask your sadness or even your true feelings in the moment, it's simply a way to help others remember that there are people in the world making a difference and changing lives for the better. Perhaps in sharing that news, you'll be able to realize that message for yourself as well.

CHAPTER 3

Managing and Overcoming Rejection

"TO HAVE FAITH IS TO TRUST YOURSELF
TO THE WATER. WHEN YOU SWIM,
YOU DON'T GRAB HOLD OF THE WATER,
BECAUSE IF YOU DO YOU WILL SINK
AND DROWN. INSTEAD YOU RELAX,
AND FLOAT." –ALAN WATTS

COMING TO TERMS WITH FAILURE

I want you to take a moment to think about some of the decisions you've made in your life and how they've worked out: crushes you've asked out, classes where you've decided to work hard in school, friendships you've let go of because you two no longer connected. We're always making decisions in our lives; sometimes those decisions work out in our favor and sometimes they don't. There are times when we can't even anticipate what the result of our actions might be and other times when we overthink the outcome for hours on end, hoping we've made the right call and that everything will work out just fine.

No matter what the situation may be, however, we're always hoping to avoid failure of any kind, because failure for most of us means we've done something wrong. Have you ever encountered failure firsthand and found that the first thought that ran through your mind was, *Why didn't I try harder?* or *What's wrong with me, why can't I do it?* It's hard for us to look at failure as an actual marker of learning—we believe failure is impossible unless there was something in the equation we could have done better to change it all. Normally, we blame ourselves for our failures, and a large reason for that is because we have attached expectations to the task and assumed we'd be able to carry it out flawlessly.

But the major problem there is that no matter how much you reflect, there's no guarantee it's going to play out how you want it to. Let's say, for example, that there's a cute girl you've spotted at school and you want to talk to her. You see her almost every day, and anytime you do, you think of a million scenarios for how you could talk to her—what the two of you would say to each other, and how things would work out just like you'd planned. But as you see her walk on by, you stop yourself from doing it, and you let her keep moving along. *What was it that held you back?* Did you end up thinking of endless types of scenarios for how it could go wrong? Did you feel like it just wasn't the right time, that you would be bothering her, or that you just wouldn't get the words out right?

What likely held you back was some form of fear of failure. When we're trapped in our own heads, it's easier and safer to come up with the ways we could do something wrong in advance. Because of this, when it comes time to implement our plans into real life, we feel overwhelmed and doubt ourselves. For something as simple as walking up to your crush and saying hello, it becomes this complex process that makes us feel like if we're missing something—if we fail at doing things right, then we're not going to be acceptable, and we're just not good enough for them. This level of self-doubt, insecurity, and lack of confidence all comes back to not wanting to make a mistake.

Why are we so scared of it? We all have a built-in fight-or-flight response to help us better manage stressful situations, but what would it take to overcome that? To be able to turn that switch off, or better yet, to understand when it's happening so we can better control it? I think to get to that level of mindfulness, it would take a great deal of practice and hard work—but there's something much smaller that we can do right now to help battle our fear of failure and start working toward our own success.

We need to accept that everyone makes mistakes.

Not just you, everyone. Your crush makes mistakes, your parents make mistakes, your friends make mistakes, and even I make mistakes. There's not a person on the planet that has it all figured out, and the sooner you realize that, the easier it's going to be to accept that you're not alone on the path toward finding yourself and embracing your awkward. I remember as a kid, I always used to consider my parents to be two people who knew what they were doing all the time. Whenever a hardship arose, they somehow had a way of fixing it. As children, we all tend to think this way in some degree. We trust the people who raised us, who guided us, and who taught us how to handle stressful situations and the worst of all possible failures.

But then you get older and start to realize that even these people are just doing the best they can with what they know, and this can lead you in two different directions. One is that it makes you feel incredibly vulnerable and fearful of what can happen in life. *If not even they can have it together, what chance do I stand?* The other direction is to feel emboldened by the thought that even though things have not always worked out exactly how they were planned, we are all still at the point where we are today, and that point is pretty good. The idea that it may be possible to move past your mistakes becomes all the more real to you.

The biggest truth you can learn is, despite whatever failure or hardship might fall into your lap, as long as you are alive, as long as you are breathing, and as long as you are capable of getting up and moving forward, you are not defeated. It's normal for our minds to make us feel as if failure will lead to the collapse of everything we know and love, but that's just our way of protecting ourselves from getting hurt. Is getting hurt such a bad thing, though? No one puts themselves out there in the world to get hurt on purpose, but is going into a situation knowing that there's a chance of failure and encountering that failure such a horrible thing?

FEELING LIKE YOU'RE NOT GOOD ENOUGH

•

"THE TRUTH IS: BELONGING STARTS WITH SELF-ACCEPTANCE. YOUR LEVEL OF BELONGING, IN FACT, CAN NEVER BE GREATER THAN YOUR LEVEL OF SELF-ACCEPTANCE, BECAUSE BELIEVING THAT YOU'RE ENOUGH IS WHAT GIVES YOU THE COURAGE TO BE AUTHENTIC, VULNERABLE, AND IMPERFECT."

–BRENÉ BROWN

•

Let's say you're getting ready for a job interview after getting your college degree—your whole life in school has led you to this moment. This is a point in your life where you put your skills to the test and showcase your merit, with the hope that the person thinking about hiring you will see how good you are. In your mind you're hoping for the best, but there's always that hint of doubt that tells you that maybe you're not good enough; maybe you don't have what it takes to get this job. Then, after waiting for a response from them following your interview—with the anticipation of a few days or weeks seeming like a few months or years—they tell you they're going to have to pass. Alternately, (what may more realistically happen,) they don't respond to you at all because they don't have the time to notify all the candidates they aren't accepting.

That might feel soul-crushing and as if your hard-earned education was all for nothing. However, despite that door closing, you still have the same level of knowledge you did before, and you are still the same person, despite being overlooked by just one potential employer. There exists a space in between knowing and not knowing something—a space that we can either fill up with doubt, or fill up with empowerment. That space is right before you open that letter from the school saying whether you got accepted or not, right before you open that email letting you know you were hired, or right before your crush responds to you asking them out or your parents tell you something important. If you choose to fill that space with empowerment, then your focus shifts from feeling nervous to knowing that no matter what comes next, you will be able to handle it. If you let your doubts creep in, then they might prevent you from even acting next time—you may give up before you even start, to avoid the potential pain you may encounter—and this isn't a healthy state to be in.

So let's say you choose empowerment. You choose not to let the outcome dictate how you will choose to handle it. It sounds like a pretty big task, doesn't it? The thing is, it's easier than you think. Once you start to reshape your mindset to see the world happening *with* you rather than *to* you, you'll get better and better at recognizing that no matter what happens, you're still here and you still have the chance to shape it in the way that you want. For a while now, we've been talking mainly about shaping your own path, but there's another piece to it all that we have to take into account here: other people.

We don't exist in a singular vacuum all by ourselves. We live with other people, and no matter how much we think we can control our own reactions, we are powerless to control the reactions of others. And this is where it can get pretty hard, mainly because no matter how much you want other people to see things your way, there's no guarantee that it will ever happen. Everyone has their own story and experiences, and the skills you've gained over the years in tackling those failures aren't the same ones that other people have built, which is why it's so tricky. Let's say for example that you and a friend are planning on going to a party together. Along the way, however, you end up taking too much time getting ready, or you forget where the address is—just some of the possible reasons why someone would be running late. In your mind, you might feel a little nervous about being embarrassed for showing up late or for just not sticking to the time you said you'd be there. As you process those feelings, you can *also* tell yourself that this is a moment that will pass, and that there will be opportunities for you to sort it out. That thought can feel quite comforting, it can even change your whole perspective in the process of getting ready.

You might not stress out about what you're wearing, you might not constantly check your phone to calculate your timing—you might simply be at peace and ready to tackle the outcome when you get there. Your friend however, may not. In fact your friend may handle things in a completely opposite way. They may start being passive aggressive, blame you for taking too long, become disgruntled with traffic slowing you both down, or feel angry at the host for not starting the party later in the night. All of their reactions are out of your hands. The best thing you can do in that moment is gain control over how you feel rather than letting their feelings take control of you.

And that's quite hard to do, don't get me wrong. It's often the people we're closest to who have the easiest time pushing our buttons the most effectively. With strangers, we don't know enough about them to feel like we have them all figured out. With our relatives and our friends, however, we've generally known them for so long that we think of their characteristics and reactions as intrinsic to their overall personality, which makes us skeptical about their ability to change. Yet for some reason, we always gravitate toward the idea of telling those close to us what they are doing wrong and how they can handle the situation better. Learning to change that approach is necessary, though, if we want to stop being stuck in our expectations of how they react, which ultimately can control how we feel in the end.

Why then does it hurt so much when we fail to meet the expectations of others? Why do we have trouble treating things as no big deal, or as something we can manage, when it comes to *other* people sharing their feelings about us? Failure isn't something that rests on the shoulders of one person. Failure can trickle down and affect everyone around you, and your natural instinct might be to limit the amount of collateral damage in the wake of your letting someone down. Sometimes we wish we could even go back in time to prevent the whole thing from happening. No one wants to experience the sheer disappointment of someone they care about feeling hurt by something they did. But that's not reality. You can't anticipate everything that's bound to happen, and more than that, you can't dictate how other people should process your failure.

That's why it is so essential to practice gratitude for the things you have, the people you have, and the opportunities that lie ahead of you. You can't repeat the past, and you can't reverse something that has already happened—you simply need to pick up your suffering and bear it. Better days will always be ahead as long as you are still alive.

We all have done things that we regret and have hurt people in ways we didn't intend to, but we can't allow that to be the excuse that holds us back from improving and trying again. Now is your moment to embrace your past, to embrace the missteps and the hardships, and to move forward in a way that shines a light wherever you go.

THE LESSON BEHIND BEING TOLD "NO"

•

"USUALLY WHEN WE HEAR OR READ SOMETHING NEW, WE JUST COMPARE IT TO OUR OWN IDEAS. IF IT IS THE SAME, WE ACCEPT IT AND SAY THAT IT IS CORRECT. IF IT IS NOT, WE SAY IT IS INCORRECT. IN EITHER CASE, WE LEARN NOTHING."

–THICH NHAT HANH

•

One of the most destructive and enlightening words a person can be told is "no." It can shut down any hope we have to succeed in our aims, and it can make us feel like we're not good enough—that we are fools for even attempting to try something outside of our comfort zone. However, it can also be exactly what we need to hear to get motivated. It can push us to prove to ourselves that as long as we have a will, we will find a way.

Think about the last time someone told you no. If you look closely at their reason why, you'll see it usually falls into one of two categories. The first is that they said no because they didn't want you to do something revolving around them. In cases like this, it might be a person asserting their own boundaries and letting you know what they feel comfortable with. For example, if you're talking to a person you like and you begin to flirt with them in a way that may be too much for them, they may tell you "no" to stop it so that they don't feel uncomfortable. It's always a good thing to listen to other people about how they feel so you can approach a situation with confidence. They may not be saying "no" with the intention to hurt you but merely to relay how they feel.

This can be a major learning moment if you remember *why* it's being said. Shift the focus away from insecure feelings that they're rejecting you because "you're not good enough." A good way to practice handling a situation like this is to take a moment before you respond to reflect on why they may have said "no" to you. Most of the time we're quick to respond out of hurt rather than understanding because it creates a safeguard for us. If someone denies us something, we find it easier to proclaim that there is something wrong with *them* and that it's an issue they need to work out. Sometimes that may be true, but the other half we're forgetting is that we also need to work on handling *hearing* "no."

After you have taken that moment before responding to think about their perspective, remember that most people do not have evil intentions when they assert something. They simply want to let you know what their boundaries are. Realizing this can only help you achieve better communication with them. In moments like these, validation for that other person is important, because it allows them to recognize that you don't see their assertion as a form of rejection. You can validate someone's response by saying, "Thank you for sharing how you feel. I really appreciate you doing that here." This isn't to say you agree with what they are saying, but it does show that you are willing to understand it. Being able to validate the feelings of others and not misinterpret their behaviors as intentional attacks on you and your character will allow them to open up more to you in the future, creating a more trustworthy and safe environment for you both.

The second category is when someone tells you "no" because they don't want you to do something for yourself. In this case, it's a little more difficult to decipher why someone would do this, but one of the most common reasons is because people are not used to others changing. We're comfortable with people staying exactly how we've always known them to be. When we see them starting to make changes, we begin questioning if we should be changing in our own lives too. Have you ever seen a friend take on a new job, move to a different city, or get engaged (just to name a few common changes) and started thinking about your own circumstances and comparing them to theirs? It's a common reaction to have, and it's totally normal to feel that way, however, it's also important to realize that just the same way you do that, other people do it too. So when you are making progressive moves in your life, it's a normal reaction for other people to be skeptical, worried, or even doubtful that you will succeed.

They may ask you lots of questions to see if you're prepared, or they may not want anything to do with you if they feel you've changed as a person. As you move through life, these reactions of rejection can become more and more common, but don't see them as obstacles. They are simply ways for you to reshape your world so that it's leaner, more efficient, and more in line with your overall goals. Where things get tricky is whether you decide to listen to the naysayers. For every new decision we make, there is a mixture of luck, bravery, and faith all tied into the outcome. We may be making the best decision of our lives, but the doubters and the haters just don't see things like we do. Or alternatively, we may be making the worst decision of our lives and our concerned friends and family are trying to protect us. How do we know when someone's rejection is worth heeding and whether their negative opinion is right?

The best way to determine a person's true feelings is to ask deeper questions about how they came to their opinion on the matter. For most people, if they simply don't want you to do something, their line of reasoning won't be as solid. If you pay close enough attention, you will be able to determine whether they're speaking from a place of concern or discouragement. For example, let's say you want to start your own podcast, and you plan on reaching out to online influencers to be guests on it. If you shared that idea with a friend and they then told you it was a bad idea and it wasn't going to turn into anything, try to get to the root of why they believe that. You may automatically start asking yourself: Do they think it's because you're not appealing enough to be able to reach people? Do they think you're not someone who can stick with something and make it work? Do they feel like you're just not entertaining enough to draw an audience?

Each of those questions, however, is coming from a place of doubt, and none of them has to do with the quality of your work or the challenge of making the podcast itself. It is easy for someone hearing those statements to feel that maybe they're true—that maybe you *aren't* good enough. But that's exactly why it is necessary to look more deeply into a person's words to see where they are really coming from. Perhaps the doubter attempted something similar to your goal and failed at it. Alternately, perhaps they just do not want to see you succeed. Either way, there is a lesson to be learned in being told "no"— listen and learn, but remember that only you can make the decision to stop doing something. No matter what anyone else says, the choice is yours and the power to make the final decision is in your own hands.

CHAPTER SUMMARY + EXERCISES

In this chapter we talked about rejection and how it can play a major role in how much time and energy you invest into certain things. We give so much power to the opinions of others, and we look for their approval to determine our own worth in this world. Hopefully, after exploring the ideas in this chapter, you can feel a little bit more at ease with not worrying too much about what others have to say.

But just to help you put these concepts into practice, there are a few things you can do to help you get real responses from other people that will test your ability to stand under the pressure of rejection. How much each individual can manage may differ, so you will personally have to decide the size of the small step you feel you can do. Nevertheless, it's a small step you should aim to take, even if the other side may seem scary.

SIGN UP FOR SOMETHING THAT HAS AN END GOAL IN MIND

Taking on new challenges should never be built on empty goals. That's why you should sign up for something where you can measure your performance at the end of a set period of time. Examples of something you may want to sign up for could include a dance class, a swimming competition, a musical performance, a stand-up comedy show, or anything where you will have to put your skills to the test. Having something to work toward will help you manage your time a lot more effectively, because you'll be looking for ways to practice monthly, weekly, or even daily.

Another piece of it all is accepting that you may just be setting yourself up for failure. Trying out something new and making a commitment to display what you've learned opens up the door for you to be imperfect. You work to display your best efforts, but when you're a beginner, it's all you can do other than waiting until you've become a complete master to share it with the world. Far too often we hold ourselves back from putting what we have out there—our working draft, our unfinished copy, our imperfect piece. Committing to this challenge can be the moment where we push past the compulsion to continue editing until we've reached the "right version" and to demonstrate what we have so far.

When the time comes for you to finally put what you have on display, do it proudly without the fear of failing. Because even if you do fail, you can proudly say you took on a brand new challenge. You dedicated time, effort, and energy to making it happen, which is not something many other people can say. **The only options you have in**

front of you are to win or to learn. Once you overcome this challenge, you'll start to see that the next one you take on will follow the same pattern: the fear of failure, the willingness to succeed, and the accomplished feeling of applying yourself as best you can.

5 PEOPLE, 5 EXPECTATIONS, 5 CHANGES YOU WANT TO BE ACCEPTING OF

The expectations we have of others can feel rewarding when they are met, but can also be damaging when we hold on to them after that person fails to uphold them. This is where overthinking becomes a prominent factor in how we see the role of others in our lives. We build up the idea of how we expect them to behave, how we want them to interpret what we say, and how we want them to respond when we don't display our best behavior. That's why if you want to move beyond feeling like you're not good enough, it has to start with identifying the expectations that keep you reaching for more. Once we know what they are, we can start to work on letting them go.

With that said, I want you to think of five people in your life that you hold in a very high regard. Each one can be a family member, a teacher, a friend, or even just someone you respect. Try to keep it to people with whom you have frequent interactions, because those are the only relationships you can realistically work on. Once you've outlined the five people you turn to for advice, lean on for support, or admire for their sense of character, think of five expectations you hold because of those people.

Do you expect any of them to always be honest with you, no matter what? Do you expect any of them to think about your feelings first and foremost when something arises? Do you expect any of them to apologize first when the two of you have a disagreement or an argument? Taking note of what your expectations are will allow you to realize why these people are important to you. Think about these expectations and why you hold them. Have the people you've chosen always upheld them? What do you tend to feel when they don't?

Now that you know what your expectations of them are, think about five positive reactions you would want to have when they do not meet your expectations. For example, if you expect your parents to always be honest with you, but you encounter a situation where you found out they did lie, how could you respond to that type of situation in a way where you could be more accepting of them? What would that look like for you?

Mapping out a strategy doesn't always mean you'll follow through in that exact way, but it does help you see what the larger picture looks like, and in gaining that perspective, you'll see that there are ways to handle feeling let down by someone else—ways that don't take any toll on what your true worth is. Because in the end, your true worth is only determined by you.

EXPLORE THE NEXT "NO" YOU RECEIVE

Usually when we hear the word "no" from someone, we take it as something final. We think that the other person's mind is made up and the best thing we can do is to let that part of our life go without ever looking back on it. Looking back might mean reliving past hurt, and that's something we want to avoid at all cost. But what if instead of running away from the dark, we aimed to shed light on it?

The next time someone tells you "no," make it your goal to break down their "no" in a way that is kind and compassionate toward them. Simply asking the person "why" won't cut it, so try to explore a bit more deeply than that by finding out what emotional factors played into their decision. For example, let's say you have a crush on someone that you've been talking to for a while. The time finally comes where you feel comfortable enough to ask them to hang out one-on-one, but when you do, they tell you that they would prefer that the two of you just remain friends.

From the perspective of finding a romantic relationship perspective, it might make sense to let it be and move on, but from a learning perspective, you can always ask that person, "What was it about the way I interacted with you that made you feel that way?" Exploring their response (if they are willing to provide one) will help you learn how to manage the next situation a lot more effectively. Plus it helps you start to reshape rejection as not something you have to run away from but something you can learn from.

Chances are you might run into some situations where the other person may not want to talk about why they said no. Either way, though, nothing is lost by simply asking. You are showing them that you're willing to put your ego aside so that you can work on being a better person, that you're the kind of person who is aware you are still discovering yourself, and that feedback is something that is welcomed, not shunned.

CHAPTER 4

Understanding Compassion

"COMPASSION IS BY DEFINITION
RELATIONAL. COMPASSION LITERALLY
MEANS 'TO SUFFER WITH,' WHICH
IMPLIES A BASIC MUTUALITY IN THE
EXPERIENCE OF SUFFERING. THE
EMOTION OF COMPASSION SPRINGS
FROM THE RECOGNITION THAT THE
HUMAN EXPERIENCE IS IMPERFECT."

–KRISTIN NEFF

SELF-COMPASSION IS THE ROOT OF ALL HAPPINESS

Compassion is a funny word. Usually when we use it we tend to see compassion as something we offer to others but rarely ever apply to ourselves. We observe the emotions of others and respond to them, all the while feeling like we're approaching situations with an aligned and sensible perspective. It then becomes an easy task for us to jump into someone else's predicament with our own experiences and try to figure out how we would manage their situation. Have you ever done that before? Have you ever spent time with a friend who was down because they were single or because they failed a test and found that you put yourself in their shoes emotionally? In some ways, this is a method for us to subtly reflect on our own circumstances and realize that things may not be as bad as we would think.

Offering compassion to other people is a generous gift, however, it's when we practice self-compassion that we can start to develop a life where we feel happy and comfortable about who we are. To practice self-compassion means to approach situations from a place of non-judgment. Whenever we make a mistake, say something wrong, fail an assignment, forget something important, or just spend too much time in our heads overthinking a negative outcome, we can end up becoming our own harshest critics. We notice the pieces of the puzzle that others don't see, pick them apart, and tear ourselves down. Being able to approach ourselves with non-judgment is to recognize that we are simply human and trying our best.

No one walks through life automatically knowing how to handle situations that are beyond their grasp. Some of us may be better at resolving them temporarily, but the skill of looking back in a non-judgmental way requires practice and awareness. We have to recognize the factors that caused what happened, what we should have taken into account, and most importantly, what we can do differently next time. Answering these questions, especially in the moment right after something happens, is the hardest thing to do. It seems almost instinctual for most of us to look around to others involved and to await their say on how lightly or how harshly we should be judged. If a person responds in a loving and caring way, we may end up going easier on ourselves. If they respond in a negative and harsh way, we may feel like their anger is justified and that their words are truth to power.

What if there was another way, though? What if people's opinions don't have to determine how we react? What if we simply accepted that others see the world from their own experiences—just like we do? Wouldn't it then become easier for us to recognize our own shortcomings as learning experiences? I hope that would be so. But, in order to reach that frame of mind, we need to start with the everyday moments we experience and practice self-compassion in its simplest form.

You must never ever forget that you are special, just the way you are. If you can hold on to that idea, then you can approach anything knowing that you carry the infinite wisdom of the personal journey that you have taken. There has never been and there never will be another person quite like you. Generally we ignore this idea, we see ourselves as just like everyone else and believe that the only way to be special is to prove our worth in some way. If only we could turn that thought around; if only we could see the ultimate potential each of us have. When you look back at your life and reflect, try to see just how many times you've made a decision that has prevented your entire world from collapsing.

There is a time and place for criticism, but criticism can become counterproductive when we beat ourselves up about our shortcomings. As illustrated by the many examples I've mentioned before, falling into a cycle of negativity only perpetuates more negativity. The only solution is to embrace the awkward situations and to allow ourselves the time to process, learn, and move forward so that we can analyze what went wrong from a place of self-compassion. The internal voice in your head will probably disagree. It might tell you that you didn't try hard enough, that you are just not good enough, or that the situation at hand might not even be something you should worry about.

In the last example, our mind is trying to protect us, but in the process it can sometimes keep us from a growth experience. For example, let's say you promised a friend you would pick them up at the airport after a long cross-country flight, but suddenly you get overwhelmed with last minute tasks that set you back about an hour longer than you expected. On the car ride over, you will probably start to think of all the possible ways the outcome could have turned out better had you done something differently beforehand. If only you were more aware, intelligent, or considerate of your friend, you wouldn't have been so late.

You might also start to worry that your friend will be upset with you, that they won't be able to trust you, or even worse, that they won't be willing to hear your explanation. Whenever we encounter situations where we feel that people won't accept us, the root of it starts with us not accepting ourselves. Instead of looking at the situation as something irreparable, try to remember that you only made a mistake. You will own up to it, make it up to your friend, and remember so that it does not happen again next time. Most importantly, you have to remember that your frustration is part of the human condition. Neither this moment nor any other moment will define you. These moments only make up some parts of your life, they don't make you who you are. As long as you can walk away reflecting in a compassionate way, you have everything you need to keep moving forward in life.

One thing we can't do if we want to grow is to shut out our negative feelings and emotions completely. The least productive thing you can do for your growth is to assume that every action you take is beneficial and that whatever the result may be, everyone, including yourself, should just deal with it. Balancing how we view our actions and taking in the good along with the bad, while still maintaining compassion for ourselves, will always be a challenge. Practicing mindfulness is a way for us to observe awkward situations with a sense of balanced clarity. We do not focus on outsiders shaping our perception. Instead we try to first see things as they are before we apply our own critique and judgment to the mix.

When you start approaching uncomfortable situations with more clarity, you won't be held down by your anger and resentment when things don't work out. In fact, you will be exercising your ability to understand and connect with what you are experiencing. Eliminate the need for perfection and you will come to realize that in most cases, most people are doing the best that they can. With this knowledge, our time and attention will be better focused, not just for others' benefit but for our own as well.

Self-compassion is the root of happiness, because when we have a deep and true love for ourselves, and when we are able to accept who we are and who we choose to be, we can extend that to others and not be tied down to negative comments, negative outlooks, or negative paths that lead us astray. The only self we should therefore put on display is our honest self, the honest self that recognizes that we are flawed but still loveable for who we are. There is no need to be "good enough" by the standards of others, you simply have to be open to learning and growing if you want to tap into your own happiness.

PRACTICING COMPASSION WITH THOSE WE DON'T LIKE

•

"LOVE ISN'T A STATE OF PERFECT CARING. IT IS AN ACTIVE NOUN LIKE STRUGGLE. TO LOVE SOMEONE IS TO STRIVE TO ACCEPT THAT PERSON EXACTLY THE WAY HE OR SHE IS, RIGHT HERE AND NOW."

–FRED ROGERS

•

No matter how hard you try to always be calm and rational, there will be moments when the actions and behaviors of other people will break you out of your balanced mindset and leave you with emotions that you may not want or welcome. This can be really frustrating to deal with, even to the point where you want to lash out at them for not being kind or considerate. In these moments, we tend to forget how much control over our own emotions we truly have and what we can do to work through the situation. Usually, we focus on the negative and find that experience comforting. **It is easier to be angry than to be compassionate, it is easier to be annoyed than to be content.**

And the reason for this is because we are simply looking for emotions to guide us through our experiences. Let's say for example that you're hanging out with a group of your friends and one of them decides to make a joke about the way you look, making everyone around you laugh along and leaving you feeling like no one respects you or accepts you for who you are. In that moment, you may feel sad because they just don't get you, or hurt because you trusted those people to be on your side, or even disconnected from them because you no longer want to be around people who make you feel this way. Your mind is going to attach itself to whatever you feel, regardless of whether these emotions are good or bad. Once this happens, and even when the situation is over, you will most likely continue to ruminate on those feelings because it's much more comforting to think about what happened than it is to move on from it.

The thing is, it's important for us to reflect on our experiences and to learn from them. This prepares us for the future and what's to come, in order to make sure we don't repeat the same mistakes or create them for ourselves again. But the real issue is *how* we reflect on those instances. To use the example I mentioned above, when someone says something about us that we don't like, it is easier for us to see their words as a sign of who *we* are instead of a sign of who *they* are. These are the moments where the door opens for us to practice compassion for others, to truly take a step back and reflect on how their actions teach us what they need to work on and how they can improve in being their best self.

Think about it ... have you ever seen a happy person make fun of someone else? Would a happy person go out of their way to put someone down, talk badly about others, or even approach the world with a pessimistic and rotten attitude? Those actions are not those of someone who feels content. If you are happy with yourself and your life, you'll recognize that you have the power to uplift others, not put them down. You have the power to inspire others with your words, not make them feel worthless. And if you're truly a happy person, you'll recognize that the world is troubled and flawed, but still aim to act nobly and achieve the highest good possible.

The person who falls short of this shows that they have much to work on, and when they direct their negative attitudes toward you, practicing compassion with them is the best thing we can do to help. The compassionate path is the one that helps us understand why something is happening to us. It leads us down a path of peace rather than violence. The most common response is thinking that being compassionate toward someone who is angry, violent, rude, or mean is allowing them to get away with their actions. We can often feel as if recognizing that this person is still just human, regardless of what they have done, is like standing down and letting them get away with their behavior.

If there is a lesson to be taught and no student to learn, though, no one will grow from the experience. When we try to teach someone by allowing our negative emotions to determine how we react, we are no longer in control of the situation. For example, if you were driving a car and someone cut you off in traffic, your first reaction might be to reduce that person's humanity to that of a negative word like "idiot" or "jerk." You might think that they are stupid, incompetent, reckless, careless, or just plain clueless to what they were doing. You also may try to teach them a lesson by honking incessantly or even driving close to them to yell at them or scare them on the road. But in those instances, how often do we stop to think about what the path to peace may be?

How much time and energy do we spend thinking about what's truly important in that moment: your safety, the safety of the other cars around you, and even the safety of the driver who cut you off? Do we think about why that person may have done it? Maybe they were in a rush to somewhere important, maybe they were having a really bad day, maybe there was an emergency, or maybe they really were just being reckless. We may never know someone's true motives, but the fact that we don't have it all figured out leaves room for us to be understanding and compassionate.

The real test we face is turning this type of reaction into a consistent habit for ourselves. Letting go of the snap judgment and snap decision in favor of an awareness centered more in the present will give us a fuller picture in these situations. This task definitely isn't something you can achieve overnight. You have to work on it daily with all the people around you. When it comes to strangers, doing this might be a little bit easier, because since we don't know their backstory, it's easier to be less influenced by their actions. In most cases, we won't ever know, because we may never see them again.

Alternately, practicing with strangers might be a little bit harder for you. Perhaps you think back to a moment where a stranger provoked you and you didn't like the way you responded. This experience might have ended up staying with you and causing you to overthink the situation relentlessly.

In other cases, the real trouble may come from the people who are the closest to you. When family members or friends act in a way that you don't like, it can be harder to practice compassion with them because you know them too well. We grow up with our family and friends, and because of that, we grow used to their patterns and behaviors, which often can lead us to feel that it's impossible or unrealistic that they will ever change. When we start to think and feel this way, we toss aside the need for compassion and fall into the cycle of negativity rather than proactivity.

There needs to be an intermediate step in between others' actions and our reactions if we plan on assessing these situations through a new lens. We will need to look deeply inside our emotions and feelings while in the moment, because this is when we can recognize what we're feeling and why we're feeling it. If we are able to openly accept that we feel hurt, we can then think about why we feel hurt, followed by who was a part of that process, and finally what truly drove them to do it. Going through each of these steps builds a narrative and shows that our reactions stem from something deeper. Each of our actions and responses play off of the world around us and our past experiences, so the more we can learn to tap into what causes us to react in the way we do, the easier it will be to remember that others are doing the same when they act. Remember, we all aim to be loved and understood. The people provoking you are no different, they might just be further removed from that realization than you are. Because of that, it's important to practice compassion, not just for them, but for yourself.

APPROACHING THE WORLD WITH A COMPASSIONATE LENS

•

"WHEN ANOTHER PERSON MAKES YOU SUFFER, IT IS BECAUSE HE SUFFERS DEEPLY WITHIN HIMSELF, AND HIS SUFFERING IS SPILLING OVER. HE DOES NOT NEED PUNISHMENT; HE NEEDS HELP. THAT'S THE MESSAGE HE IS SENDING."

–THICH NHAT HANH

•

If you want to make a change in this world, the best place to start is with the resources you have right in front of you. When we think about change, we may tend to envision it on a large and global scale where everything in our existence comes into complete alignment without error, without struggle, and without rejection. But life isn't that simple. Life is complicated, messy, and confusing, and it almost always comes with just enough of a hassle that we feel like it's impossible to set the right course in this world.

Maybe the problem isn't our desire to make an effort, maybe the problem is simply that the goal is too large for us to handle all on our own. When you're young, you may sometimes feel like anything is possible, or that being a dreamer is all it takes to succeed in this world—being a dreamer gives the world a soul. But as you get older and encounter more pain and hardship, you'll start to see that the world also needs realists to keep it alive. It can be really hard sometimes to accept this since whenever we see corruption in the world, our first thought may be to step up and rid the world of it. Often we want to do all we can to eliminate the threat, the pain, and the suffering.

But life is first and foremost about discovering your power, harnessing it, wielding it, and then teaching the resulting insights to others. And even though you may feel like you're ready to jump into the gray to solve the world's problems, life is a bit more complicated than that. You might feel inclined to pick sides at times, to see one group as the good group and one as the bad, to consider one opinion truthful and another as false, one political group as crazy and one as sane, or one reality as the only reality that makes sense. How do you manage all of it? How do you know who to trust and who to listen to? Who is trying to use you, and who is trying to help you? When should you lean on others and when should you go it alone?

What I've learned in life is that it's important to determine which lens you want to employ to see the world and use that as a way to approach life and the situations you encounter. In crafting your lens, you should approach it by asking three simple questions to start, because it's on the backs of these three questions that you'll know what the noblest path is to follow; you can then make that your shining light when you encounter the vast uncertainty in the world.

QUESTION #1: WHO DO I WANT TO HELP IN THIS WORLD?

There are so many people in this world trying their best to get by and working incredibly hard to provide for their families, to gain acceptance among their friends, and to feel like they are worth it just as they are right here and now. Spending time thinking about who you want to help will narrow down what's you see is missing in this world and where you can fit into all of it. No matter where you look, no matter who you ask, one thing that you will always see that the world can use more of is compassion.

We know for ourselves that we need to be understood and cared for, but there simply isn't enough of that to go around. People can get so wrapped up in their worlds that they tend to forget what it means to treat others with respect, kindness, and care. By approaching the world with a lens of compassion, you'll start to see who you can help in this world.

Sometimes it may end up being your family members who just can't seem to get along after long, stressful school and work days. In those situations, approach them with compassion. Let them know that you understand that times may feel tough for them, but that you're there to help them get through it, and that they aren't alone in this world.

Maybe other times it's strangers that you meet online, people who feel the need to "troll" conversations or say harsh things to and about others because they themselves are hurting inside and they don't have any other way to express themselves. Take the time to see beyond their harsh comments and ask them how they are doing. Hopefully, they'll be able to open up to you, but if not, you'll know that at least you opened the door for them to see that there are good people out there willing to help.

Recognizing who you can help will lead you to discover your own natural and inherent powers. You will discover that the good you have deep inside of you can make a difference even on the smallest of levels. Also, that you have the power to help other individuals change, and finally, to change yourself.

QUESTION #2: WHAT SKILLS DO I HAVE TO DO IT?

It's common to feel like you're not ready or don't have what it takes to help someone else. You may feel that they need a "real" professional, someone who is highly experienced, instead of you—someone who is just learning what they can. But one simple thing to remember is that we all start at different points, and where you are today may be far ahead of where someone else is right now. Every small step you take is a teachable moment for you, something you can pass on to others on their own journeys.

Practicing compassion has no beginning and no end to it. It is as effective at the beginning as it will be at the end. So whether you know how to provide the right kind of therapy to help someone work through a tragic situation or can only sit with someone while they feel what they feel—both actions can make a world of difference to a person in need. It's time to stop just believing in your ability in the abstract and time to start empowering your ability to make real and meaningful change.

Outside of this book, there are lessons you can learn from sitting on the grass for one minute that can change your whole existence. That's why to be a great teacher means also being a mindful student, one who is always learning and always willing to grow. When it comes to skills, in a very practical sense, you may not feel up to a task compared to someone who has spent their entire life studying a field, but that's where you can lean on them to learn.

As we mentioned before, overcoming rejection and being able to turn to others for help and guidance is how you will expand your skills and take the measure of the power you have. You carry your entire life experience, your hurdles of dealing with rejection, and your recovery through failure in every word you speak. You have all the skills you need right here and right now.

QUESTION #3: HOW SOON CAN I START?

There will never be a "right moment" to begin anything. When you are willing, it will be the right moment. We tend to look at important moments in our lives as having a beginning and an end, but they never really end—life is always beginning. So when we think about how soon we can start, the truth is we are already starting. Asking the question just makes us realize it. If you know who you want to help and what skills you need to do so, it's just a matter of acting on those skills as best and as soon as you can. It's sort of like walking into a dark room filled with furniture. Turning on the light doesn't make the furniture physically manifest, it was there all along just outside of our ability to see it. In fact, when you walk into a dark room, you assume there is something already in there, even if you don't know what it may be. Something exists beyond your ability to know what it is, and determining when you should start helping others is just you turning on the light.

Just make sure to set your aims straight; start with what you can do. Take small steps, and try to fix your own world first by organizing the chaos in your life. If you can get a good handle on that, then move further and further outward. Offer help to your family, your friends, your classmates, your coworkers, your neighbors and on and on.

There will be tests that will challenge your willpower and people who will doubt you or attack you simply because you're defining your noble path, and they have yet to discover that it's possible for them too. Walking through the world with a compassionate lens can also feel isolating at times, like no one else has the ability to see things in this way, or even worse, no one wants to see with that lens. But don't ever let that be a reason to give up. You need to be a dreamer AND a realist. You need to give the world a soul AND you need to keep it alive.

CHAPTER SUMMARY + EXERCISES

In this chapter we talked about what it means to practice compassion and how to employ compassion for others even when they're negative and can really try to bring us down. Being able to gain perspective on a situation might seem useless sometimes in resolving an issue, but it plays a huge role in helping you understand it, and with that knowledge you can act with a clearer and more conscious mindset in the future. Since we all start at different places when it comes to how compassionate we are, you should look at building it up like you would a muscle.

Putting in a little training daily can help you shift to a compassionate approach before you take a non-compassionate one, which sometimes might be your first instinct. Some of us have been raised in more loving, compassionate, and understanding households, while others haven't had the best experience with others practicing compassion with them. No matter what, though, it's possible for anyone to work on this, even if you have a short temper or feel very jaded about trusting others or expecting there to be even an ounce of good in them. The change that will happen here is not intended for their benefit, although they may be a recipient of it—it's ultimately for your own.

With the exercises in this chapter, you can train your skill of compassion and get better and better at it if you really work on growing into the person you truly want to be.

CALL YOURSELF OUT ON YOUR STRONGEST NEGATIVE THOUGHT

We all have negative thoughts bubbling around in our heads, telling us we're not good enough or smart enough to do the things we want to. The first step in overcoming those negative thoughts is to identify them. Shining a light in a dark room not only can give you clarity as to what's around but can also help you move past the fear of what's unknown. So how do you figure out what your strongest negative thought is?

Consider—what is the thought that makes you the most depressed? What is the negative thought that you believe to be the most true? I would say it's the thought that pops up the most in your head. This thought may not affect you the most deeply, and you may not believe it to be the most realistic idea, but it is the one that you simply can't escape because it's worked its way into the different elements of your life. Such a thought can seem very subtle and small, but can actually be quite dangerous. The reason why it's the hardest to quell is because it often goes unchallenged—you accept it with open arms simply because it's easy to overlook.

What is that thought for you?

For some people, it may be that you're just not smart enough and that because of that, people don't take you seriously. Maybe it's a physical characteristic, and you believe because of it, people are not as interested in interacting with you. Your strongest negative thought is usually something you never verbalize, and if you do, it's probably done in a joking, self-deprecating way.

My nose is just a little too big.

I was never really good at school anyway.

I'm just a naturally awkward person.

Turn the light on that negative thought, and make it very clear that this is the one you want to release. When you know what the thought is, you can call yourself out whenever you think it—and make yourself absolutely aware that it's entered your head. Once you're able to do that, you should tell yourself that it's something you want to clear out. Even just taking that step is a huge move in the right direction—one in which you're becoming more observant and aware of what's under the radar in your own life. It also shows that you're not going to let that thought prevent you from being compassionate to yourself, and that despite this negative idea, you are still someone who matters, even if you may not quite believe it yet.

UNMASK ONE IMPORTANT DETAIL ABOUT HOW A NEGATIVE PERSON LIVES IN THEIR DAILY LIFE

There's no shortage of negative people in this world. Anywhere you go, you'll most likely encounter someone who is in a rush somewhere or is having a bad day and decides to take it out on you. It can be very frustrating to have to deal with other people's negative spirals, but it also presents an opportunity to practice compassion. **There are two steps to practicing this exercise; the first one is a test of patience and the second one is a test of action.**

If someone were to tell you beforehand that they were going to be outraged and negative, it might help you better prepare for the situation and figure out how to handle it much more effectively. However, that's likely never going to happen. When negativity strikes, it will most certainly catch us off guard and make us feel like we're swept up in the mix of it. Sometimes we will be unaware of our own reaction because it just naturally flows out in response to the situation. But whenever something happens, if you are able to remain quiet, composed, and calm, and give yourself ninety seconds to breathe in and out, then when the time comes to react, you will have a completely different approach than you did before.

The instant reaction operates based on fear, confusion, and panic. The ninety-second reaction comes more from a place of calm and clarity. Your brain has time to bring the pieces together to gain a better outlook on what has happened, and because of that, you're far more likely to remember that there's another person on the other side of the equation. How often we forget that we're dealing with other people, people who are going through their own experiences and most likely are not practicing mindfulness when they get pulled into their own world of anger.

Since you are aware, or at least trying to practice awareness, it falls on you to recognize the humanity necessary here and the compassion needed for you to best determine what's necessary to handle the situation. In trying to figure out what to do, taking those ninety seconds also makes it harder to make a snap judgment. Instead of instantly declaring that the other person is insane, stupid, or an idiot, you can ask for more information in order to learn more about them.

Try to find out what they were going through moments before the situation escalated. If you can take it one step back, they may open up and take you back even further. Eventually the picture you may start to see is that their anger was expressed to you but doesn't derive from you. Even if they're specifically angry about something you did ... what was it in their day that prepared them to feel this way? You might even be able to go further back to find out what you can do to be more compassionate.

Taking this approach doesn't guarantee that the other person will open up. They may be too caught up in their anger to even want to share anything with you. And if that ends up being the case, the most compassionate thing you can do is to recognize that they are not ready to tackle it. Respect their time and space while you focus on tackling the anger, frustration, or sadness within yourself.

LIMIT YOUR MEDIA CONSUMPTION FOR THE WEEK TO NO MORE THAN 35 MINUTES

It's easy to feel helpless when you focus on things that are out of your control. The media we consume has a habit of doing that to us. Taking in information from distant sources opens us up to things that are happening outside of our own experience, leaving us with feelings, thoughts, and questions that never really end up being resolved. And with every moment we spend on every social media platform, we are consuming content like never before.

Watching videos on YouTube, scrolling through our Facebook feeds, checking out things our friends post on Snapchat and Instagram: taking in all of this content can make you feel like you're well-rounded and informed about what's going on, but more than likely, it will leave you craving more at the end. You'll return over and over, refreshing each application to see what's new, knowing that there's *always* new things to consume. Trust me, I'm not against consuming information, as I think the world is shifting more and more in that direction, so it's best to find a way to control it rather than eliminate it.

That's why it's best to practice mindful consumption whenever we view content.

We may hear something in the news that upsets us, worries us, or even makes us feel bad about ourselves in comparison to others. And even though we experience these negative emotions, we still dive deep into the content out there, hoping that these things won't affect us. The only way to combat experiencing those feelings is to limit the amount of media you consume. By simply taking control of how much time you want to dedicate to what you watch, you'll become more aware of what you choose to spend your time on.

I would recommend five minutes a day. Allow yourself only five minutes of outside world content that has to do with news that won't play into your daily life. For example, if you're watching a news channel or listening to someone recap the news cycle for the day, pick and choose the news stories that seem the most important and let go of the rest. Setting limitations will enforce the consideration you have for what you actually end up consuming, and it will prevent you from getting sucked into the refresh cycle of it all.

What do you do, though, if in those five minutes you encounter something that disrupts your world view, or something that makes you feel helpless or worthless? This is where your compassion practices will come into play. Remember that the events happening outside of your here and now are not things you can change or control. What you do have power over are the things you can actively change. You should feel a sense of comfort in knowing you're not responsible for fixing the entire world, it's not your duty or your obligation to fix everything.

By setting a limit and choosing the things you want to consume, for five minutes a day or thirty-five minutes a week, you will gain a better sense of what's important, how to react compassionately to what happens, and finally see where you can make a *real* difference in this world.

CHAPTER 5

Creating Healthy Relationships

"BUT WHO ARE WE, REALLY? JUST
A BUNDLE OF GOOD GENES AND
BAD GENES MIXED WITH GOOD
HABITS AND BAD HABITS. AND SINCE
THERE'S NO GENE FOR COOLNESS OR
CONFIDENCE, THEN BEING UNCOOL
AND UNCONFIDENT ARE JUST BAD
HABITS, WHICH CAN BE CHANGED WITH
ENOUGH GUIDANCE AND WILL POWER."

–NEIL STRAUSS

WE'RE ALL A LITTLE SCARED OF THE PEOPLE WE'RE INTERESTED IN

Having the courage to talk to someone you like can take time and the patience to build up your confidence, courage, and conversational skills, but before I get into how and why courage is important, I first want to talk about the process of developing feelings for someone. When you spot someone who catches your eye, it's easy for your mind to wander beyond how well you actually know them into an imaginative state where things will happen exactly how you envision that they will. And there are a multitude of factors right there that might be attractive to you: the way they look, their style, their intelligence, their popularity, their wholesomeness, their flirtiness, the list goes on and on.

In the process of just looking at them, you might start to envision what it would be like if the two of you were dating, or if you two were to kiss, be together, or even just share awesome experiences with one another. The thought of that person can fill you with such a high, it can make you feel like they're perfect in your eyes and that they can do no wrong. But at some point, reality may start to hit and you may be left wondering ... *is it even possible, though? How would I even go about asking someone like that out? How would I know what to say or how to manage my nervous feelings around them? How do I keep them interested, and how often should I text them?*

Your mind starts to flood itself with questions, all of which you don't quite have the answers to, and thinking of the answers is not as fun as daydreaming about how perfect the two of you would be together. When most people think about approaching someone they like, they're hit with a jolt of fear that makes them question if taking action will leave them better or worse off here. By talking to the other person, things *could* potentially work out. Maybe you'll know exactly how to handle the situation—maybe things will work out smoothly, and they will like you back just as much as you like them. But what if they don't? What if you talk to them and you screw things up, make them hate you, or make them just feel completely awkward around you?

Everything is small steps.

If you want to be effective in talking to someone you like, you've got to take the right approach in preparing yourself so that no matter what the outcome may be, you'll feel equipped to handle it. That's why the first thing I would recommend you focus on are three key steps to help you—not only to get noticed by the person you like, but to help set the groundwork for your courage. Before we get to these three steps, however, let me address some common taboos. There are a lot of taboos that exist about girls and guys when it comes to dating. Some of them are:

- Guys should always make the first move, or else they'll be considered wimps.
- Girls should never be too loud or crazy, or else they'll turn guys off.
- Guys should keep their emotions to themselves, or else they'll look whiny.
- Girls shouldn't voice their concerns or feelings, or else they'll sound like they're nagging.

The major problem with these ideas is that they set limitations for how a person can act on the basis of how other people will perceive them. Since these taboos have become so integrated into our society, it creates pressure for people to "follow the rules" and to not express themselves too much outside of them, or else they will be criticized. Over the years I've spoken to hundreds of guys who feel the pressure to ask out their crush because not doing so would make them feel like they are chickening out, or that they are less than their worth. I've also spoken to hundreds of girls who feel like they need to lay down clues to get the guy's attention, that approaching him and asking him out isn't something that girls are supposed to do.

In order to really challenge these limiting ideas, we need to set the groundwork for how healthy relationships should work. **The three key steps you should focus on when getting in the mindset to ask someone out or get closer to a person you like are: (1) making eye contact, (2) smiling, and (3) saying hello.** In previous chapters, we talked about knowing your self-worth and putting that on display so you can be confident in who you are. That idea can totally slip your mind if you see someone you're attracted to, almost as if you're starting from scratch once again. When you focus on making eye contact with someone, you're holding that solid ground for yourself, proving that you have what it takes to be noticed and to notice someone in return.

The first key step is to make eye contact. Eye contact between two people can be a special way to bond. You both recognize one another and acknowledge that the other person sees that as well. When a person tries to make eye contact with you but you end up looking away, you're signaling your inability to show them who you are. What they end up seeing is someone who is timid, someone who is nervous, and someone who isn't ready to talk to them. I know ... sometimes it can be awkward and intimidating to hold eye contact with someone you like. But that is all the more reason why you should practice doing it with people who you do not find intimidating. If you see a friend in the hallway, hold eye contact when you talk to them; if you interact with a bus driver or someone on the street, hold eye contact when you talk to them. Practicing this small step will help you get better and better at showing the world that you are someone who is planted in the ground and is on their path to knowing themselves.

The next key step is to smile. Smiling is something that's seriously underrated, namely because we've been taught that by not smiling, you can look cooler, more sultry, and more mysterious. On the other hand, you also look uninviting and creepy (if you're making eye contact without smiling). I think you can still be suave while smiling, especially if you direct it at a person you like. When humans see other humans smile, it triggers them to smile as well. Good thoughts and feelings are passed around by everyone involved, so why *wouldn't* you want to create that atmosphere? Some of us might be a little embarrassed by our smiles, though. Maybe your teeth are not straight or you don't like the way your smile looks for another reason. The thing is, the purpose of your smile here is not to win contests or to be put on magazines, it's to express your sense of joy in seeing the person you like. If you show them that your awareness of them makes you happy, then you'll be sharing positive thoughts with them.

The third key step is to say hello. Just a simple "hi" can do wonders for making your presence known in another's eyes. In school, on the street, at work, or just about anywhere, people are always passing other people. Most of the time we are ignoring others or have our heads down and are not really thinking about interacting. In those brief moments where two people cross paths, most of the time we just let that moment go with no one really acting on it. But by saying hello, you're breaking that pattern and showing the other person that greeting them is something that matters to you, that they are worth paying attention to, and that they are not someone you want to ignore. Normally, when it comes to talking to someone new, it's easy to get tripped up over the idea of what you should actually say to them. Getting into the habit of saying a simple "hello" will keep you focused every step of the way so you don't end up avoiding the interaction all together.

When you combine all three of these steps, you will start to see that they paint the picture you may want to get across but are having trouble demonstrating. You're an inviting person, you're friendly, and you're confident enough to start the interaction with them. Even if every time you take these three steps the person doesn't hold eye contact, or smile, or say hello back, you at least know that you're building a positive habit with this behavior for yourself—which will make it much easier to do when you encounter someone you really like and are just way too scared to approach.

KEEP THE CONVERSATION GOING

•

"TO EFFECTIVELY COMMUNICATE, WE MUST REALIZE THAT WE ARE ALL DIFFERENT IN THE WAY WE PERCEIVE THE WORLD AND USE THIS UNDERSTANDING AS A GUIDE TO OUR COMMUNICATION WITH OTHERS."

–TONY ROBBINS

•

Getting a person's attention is different from holding their attention and keeping them interested in what you have to say. Beyond just saying hello and introducing yourself, you may struggle with finding the right words to keep the conversation going, which can make it far easier to use distractions to hold yourself back from acting at all. Things you may tell yourself like, "They're busy right now," "I don't know what to talk about," or "What if they don't like me?" are all excuses that build up because we are waiting too long to act on our instinct. If you were instead to see someone you want to interact with and then approach them in that same moment—without overanalyzing the situation—the outcome might surprise you.

The three-second rule is what I would recommend using to help you jump past that nervous hurdle and into the fray, where you will get a result that's not based on a what-if setup. The way the rule works is: whenever you see someone you want to talk to, give yourself no more than three seconds to approach them and start talking. If you stay in place thinking about it instead, more and more reasons will start to pop up as to why that moment simply isn't the right time. But if you count to three and then start walking toward them, you're already in motion, so there's less of a chance of you backing away from the interaction. As you get closer, you may start to feel tension, awkwardness, and failure in your wake. However, whatever the result of the experience, whether good or bad, it will ultimately leave you with something of substance and certainty.

Instead of wondering what would have happened if you had taken that chance, you will have some kind of interaction with that person, and from there you can better calibrate what to do the next time around. Each and every interaction is a way for you to learn and grow, and the more you do it, the easier it becomes. Speaking from my own experience, whenever I made it my goal to approach strangers, the first time was always the most difficult, because it carried the highest burden of uncertainty. But once I got over the first hurdle, I went into my second introduction with less fear and more experience. Because if the first person didn't respond rudely or chew my head off, it was pretty likely that the second wouldn't either.

So when you actually walk up to a person you like, what do you say that's going to catch their attention, keep their interest, and help you forget about your nervousness? There's two potential ways to approach this, and I think it's up to you to figure out what works best in each scenario.

THE TWO APPROACHES

The first approach is to begin with a question. This can be a question that is relevant to your (or their) interests, and their answer will likely give you more insight into how a person like them thinks. For example, if you're approaching a girl at your school or college, you might want to ask her if she knows any good movies to watch, places to eat, or classes she would recommend you take. Let her know that you wanted to get her opinion on the matter because you wanted to gain a female's perspective.

As she gives you her answer, you can always use the follow-up technique, which is to go deeper into your question. If she tells you to watch a horror movie, you can ask her what her favorite horror movie is, and then dig deeper again and find out if she's ever had any real-life horror or ghost story experiences. If she tells you about a burger place not too far from there, you can ask her what her favorite food is, then dig deeper again and find out what the one food she would want to eat forever on a desert island would be. No matter what type of question you ask her, there is always another layer of depth that you can explore, so try to see how much you can get that person to open up as you talk to them.

The second approach is to begin with a story. This can be something that happened to you recently or something that has been on your mind for a while. Either way, the purpose here is to showcase a safe and human side to yourself so the other person's interest is piqued to the point where they want to know all the details about what happened. With this approach, your ability to tell a good story is going to be put to the test. If you get too detailed too soon, the person may tune out what you're saying. So it's important to engage with them along the way as you tell them your story. For example, let's say there's a cute guy at your job that you want to talk to, but you just don't know what to say to him at all. If you approach him, you might want to let him know that you want to get his opinion on something that happened to you, and from there you can tell him about a dilemma that one of your friends is going through, as well as how you're trying to decide what your mission is life is, what your next big project should be, or anything that you feel comfortable sharing.

As you talk to him about your story, at any point you can always ask him if he's ever had an experience like the one you're sharing before. If he says he has, shift the conversation over to him so he can open up as well. Then keep sharing back and forth between the two of you, leading the conversation into deeper questions and more opening up. Being a good listener is key here, because you aren't simply listening to keep talking about yourself. What you are looking for are points of common ground that show that the two of you have more in common than two average strangers do, which is why it's totally fine for the two of you to keep talking.

All that person really wants in the moment when you first interact with them is to see where things will go. Both of you may be worried about how long you're going to talk, so setting up a flexible time constraint for yourself may help you stay focused so you don't feel like you're rambling on and on. Telling the other person that you have to leave in a few minutes gives them a sense of security that you're not going to stick around until things get awkward. But if you see that things aren't getting awkward and the two of you are actually connecting, you can feel free to hit the snooze button on that time constraint alarm and keep it going for a few more minutes.

Working up the skill to effectively approach and engage with a person simply takes time, but there are a few shortcuts you can use to help practice for the serious contenders you want to approach. If you're completely new to talking with strangers, I would focus your energy on talking to people who you do not find at all intimidating. This may mean striking up conversations with random people sitting with you in class, coworkers or customers at your job, people you pass in the park or the bus, or pretty much anyone who seems like a regular person to you. Like I mentioned before, the first time is always going to be the hardest since you're breaking the seal on your interactions with others, so instead of starting off talking to the person you really want to talk to, warm up with someone who can help you get into a more social mood.

If you want to approach your crush, try talking to two or three other girls or guys to whom you're not as strongly attracted and get more comfortable asking questions or sharing stories with them. If you want to make friends at a party or an event you're attending, try to strike up a conversation either with people you see waiting to get in or in more relaxed areas, like where food or drinks are being served. Keeping the conversation going only works if you are constantly in the flow of talking to new people to the point where approaching one more person—the one you're interested in—is no different from how you've done it tons of times before.

What's really cool about practicing these social interactive skills is that you don't only have to use them with people you don't know. They can also be a way for you to develop deeper connections with family members, classmates, friends, and more. Each and every person has their own unique story to tell, so if you can help them feel comfortable sharing more of that with you by sharing more of yours with them, it will strengthen that connection tremendously. Not to mention that asking questions and going deeper with family members whom you might not be as close with can nourish a bond. Showing them that you are genuinely interested in the things that make them who they are will help you practice all the other skills I've mentioned before: compassion, mindfulness, and loving-kindness (a term from Buddhism). We're all just people; some of us might be a little more intimidating than others, but no one is above being human. As long as you talk to people like they are people, you will always have the opportunity to turn that conversation into something great.

LOWER YOUR EXPECTATIONS AND MEET PEOPLE WHERE THEY ARE

Your ability to carry out conversations will improve the more you practice, but where a lot of people end up getting stuck is in how to end the conversation. If you're talking to someone new, you might contemplate asking them for their contact information, or you may just want to leave things on a positive note for a future conversation. For some, not knowing how to end a conversation could be reason enough for them to not want to have it at all. If you feel like you're one of those people who would avoid the whole interaction in order to prevent a potentially awkward ending, realize that it doesn't have to be awkward if you don't want it to be. There are ways to wind down a conversation just as there are ways to start one, and learning how to master these techniques will allow you to walk away from any interaction feeling confident in yourself and your ability to approach that person again.

Just to make it clear though, not every single person you talk to is going to want to talk to you again. There will be plenty of cases where interactions don't work out in the way that you'd prefer. However, you shouldn't see those experiences as failures. There are only two options that you can carry forward with you when it comes to breaking out of your comfort zone and trying something new—you either win, or you learn. In the first instance, the situation works itself out and you walk away feeling like you won, you accomplished your goal to talk to someone, and you did it well. Or in the alternative, it'll fall flat and things will just not move as smoothly as you wanted them to. In those cases, you learn. It's going to take some readjusting to really see it this way. Just like we talked about before when it comes to rejection—only when you've experienced it enough times can you anticipate it and prepare yourself for it.

So what exactly is the technique you should use when you're trying to end a conversation on a high note? I always recommend a compliment and a call to action. When I say a compliment, I don't mean just right off the bat telling someone that you like them or you think they're beautiful. I mean complimenting them on something that's relevant to what you two talked about. If, for example, that person had shared their favorite movie with you and then ended up telling you how they always used to watch it because it really made them light up when they were younger, your compliment can center around thanking them for opening up and sharing with you. It's incredibly rare for people to hear compliments about what they share with others, and the reason for that is we tend to give compliments on observational things like looks, status, and interests: if a guy is cute, if a girl has lots of friends, if a person is really talented at an instrument. That's where our mind generally goes, because physical observations don't need to be clarified too much, since usually they're evident to everyone there.

When you compliment someone about something they shared with you, it opens up a whole new way to explore the behind-the-scenes aspects of that person you're talking to. There are lots of different ways you can deliver a compliment, though. You can, for example, say it with sincerity:

"Thanks for opening up to me and sharing that story. You seem like a really interesting person and I would really love to get to know you better."

Or you can say it in a backhanded way, with a little sarcasm:

"You know, you're not so bad to spend time around. In fact, I think I'm actually starting to like what we have going on here. We should do this again."

However you choose to say it, the compliment should always lead into some type of call to action. A call to action is simply a way for someone to actively follow up with something in that specific moment. Instead of saying goodbye and hoping that they decide to take the next step of their own volition, you let them know right off the bat that you *want* there to be a next step and that you're telling them how to get there. In most instances, getting their number or other contact information is enough to work with. Once you have that, you can continue building the connection with them through text and eventually lead that into asking them to hang out.

What if you could use the first idea to lead to a second one? Think about it like this ... if you are trying to convince someone to cross a bridge, you can lead them to the bridge and tell them how long it is, what they will see if they look over it, and whether it's sturdy or not. In doing so, you will make them more conscious of considering actually walking on the bridge, which they may not have thought about until you put more emphasis on it. That's what generally happens when people put a lot of emphasis on getting someone's contact information. You're trying to prepare them to give you the information, but you are saving everyone the trouble just by telling them what to expect on the other side of the bridge.

Let's say that instead of telling them about the bridge at first, you tell them there is a beautiful beach that the two of you could visit. They have to cross the bridge to get there, but once you get to the beach, the two of you will have lots of fun together. In that example, the bridge is a necessary part of being able to enjoy the beach. The person won't second-guess crossing it because the reward on the other side is what they're really interested in. So when you're winding down a conversation with someone and you've already complimented them, think back to the things you talked about and base your call to action on what the two of you can do together next time. If the two of you talked about the craziest places you've ever visited before, you may want to follow up by telling them that the two of you have to find something crazy to do together. You can ask for their number so you can follow up, but keep the conversation focused on what the two of you will do. That way, giving you their number will seem incredibly natural, as if it's simply part of the process of getting to know you better.

Once you have a way of contacting them, being a good listener is essential to maintaining a good relationship with them. If you only talked to them and got their number to practice getting closer with people, make sure to establish fairly quickly that you think they could be a really awesome friend for you to have. Following up with a text or even calling them on the phone the first time might feel at first like you're starting from scratch: coming up with an opening line, worrying about holding their attention, and then finding a way to end it on a high note. What most people don't do, however, is keep the conversation going that they were previously having in person. Remember how we talked about telling them about the beach? Well, in that case, you could always start your conversation by mentioning something fun in relation to the plans you made with them.

You can make a joke about how you want to see if they'll follow through, you can send them a picture of yourself getting ready to go do that thing by yourself, or you can go deeper and try to learn more about why that thing is important to them. The key to conversation is to spin each note off from a single thread. If you're able to tie each part back to the last, it will never seem like you misspoke or changed the dynamic of the connection you two had. I mentioned listening earlier because this is another major component that is often overlooked. Sometimes when you're excited to talk to someone, you tend to fill in the excitement on the other end for them. If you really want to hang out with them, you might be overly enthusiastic and message them a lot or you might keep asking more and more questions without them giving you fun and detailed answers in response.

It's crucial to recognize where everyone is at every step of the way. Whether it's when you first say "hi" or when you're meeting up to hang out one-on-one for the first time, don't let your enthusiasm cloud your perceptions, be mindful in each moment you interact with them, and try to show honesty in how you respond. There may be moments when the other person simply doesn't want to text you, and that's OK. There may be moments where they just don't connect with you or they feel hurt or pushed away by something you said. It's impossible to anticipate every reaction or response, the best you can do is simply to be open to listening without judgment. Although you might feel hurt or slighted when a person no longer wants to talk to you or see you, take a moment to think about it from their perspective.

If you see that there's far more to the story than what you have access to or know, then you can compassionately recognize that there's more to learn and that it's too quick to draw conclusions right now. Healthy relationships involve releasing just as much as they do drawing someone in, and if you only focus on pulling someone into your world, you're going to stretch them too thin. Remember that it's OK to let people focus on themselves, think things through on their own, and respond to you when they feel ready.

CHAPTER SUMMARY + EXERCISES

In this chapter we explored what it takes to create healthy relationships with others, focusing mainly on talking to new people that you want to bring into your life. Every stranger holds an element of uncertainty; you can never quite know from the beginning whether the two of you will connect. But there are lots of different techniques you can put into play to make that interaction more natural and fluid between the two of you. As with any other kind of technique, you need to practice it over and over in order to not only become good at it, but to really fine-tune your own unique style with it.

For example, when a person wants to become a comedian and they tell a funny joke to one of their friends, the friend will see that as exactly what it is: a funny joke. By itself, the joke receives the credit, because the comedian hasn't yet established himself enough for people to see beyond the joke. However, as he continues to tell more jokes, weaving them together and keeping people's interest in what he has to say, the tone switches over to *him* being funny. People will begin to appreciate him in that situation because the jokes are simply a way for him to showcase his awesome personality—the piece of him that makes people enjoy his company and want to stick around. The exercises I've outlined below are different techniques you can practice to get better at talking to people whenever you encounter them.

At first it's going to be hard, but you'll start to see that as you do it more and more, it isn't the things you say that keep people around, it's your personality that truly shines bright enough for them to want to have a relationship with you.

TALK TO PEOPLE WITH THIS SIMPLE AND EASY GAME

Sometimes the only motivation you need to go talk to a person that you're interested in is for someone to tell you to go for it. There's a YouTube channel called *Simple Pickup* that created a game called "Go" which my friends and I adapted whenever we went out as a way to approach people without hesitating or overthinking it. The channel *Simple Pickup* focuses on teaching guys how to overcome their fears of starting conversations, asking for numbers, and overall just talking to girls. They have videos where they dressed up as Pokémon characters and used Pokémon pickup lines to start conversations, or they talked to girls while they were in wheelchairs—their videos broach every possible weird scenario you could run into, where it all comes down to confidence and how you carry yourself. Although the game is quite simple, it can be exactly what you need to get your head in the right mindset to act on your whims rather than back away from them.

When you play Go with your friends, the objective is to approach the person your friend picks out for you—to just walk right up to them to start a conversation. In some ways it can sound like Truth or Dare without the truth element, but the difference here is that if you hesitate and don't immediately approach them, you will have to do ten pushups and *then* go talk to them. Obviously no one wants to be forced to do pushups on the dirty, questionable ground and then have to go talk to someone anyway, so the incentive to do it the first time is pretty high. With Go, there is no winning or failing other than walking up to that person and talking to them. The goal is to get you out of your comfort zone and to have you do things that you didn't realize you had the confidence to do.

In reality, Go is less about the way the other person reacts and more about knowing that it's possible to talk to them. If you're in school, at a party, at the mall, or just about anywhere where there are people who are open and being social with one another, Go is the perfect game to play with your friends. There is, however, one thing that you should keep in mind when you play, and that is to remember that the idea is not to harass or bother people—it's to put yourself out there without being a jerk to others. It may be easy for your friends to point to random strangers for you to talk to because they think it's funny, but if it's not for the purpose of helping you grow as a person, then the whole game collapses on itself.

Go also gives you the opportunity to have unique experiences that you have never before imagined you would have. Beyond just approaching people you're attracted to, talking to strangers and engaging them with the techniques we've shared so far in this book, like compassionate listening, mindfulness, eye contact, and smiling, will get them to feel more comfortable opening up and talking to you. Because of that, you'll learn a lot about the people you've just met and you'll have incredibly interesting stories to share with your friends. Even the times when the person turns you down, you'll have had an in-person experience that you can reflect on to help you fine-tune how to approach the next person in a much better way.

If you want to use Go as a way to talk to your crush or someone you've been admiring for a long time, I would definitely recommend practicing with other people first. As you work on your interaction skills, Go might be the perfect way for you to finally take action and make something happen between you and someone else, something that you can be proud to say you've finally accomplished.

LEARN SOMETHING NEW, TRY SOMETHING NEW

When you're talking to someone, it can be easy to overlook the things they say out of fear or nervousness, and because of that, you might hear what they're talking about but never really take that knowledge in. An interaction is about more than just responding in a way where the other person feels like you're paying attention, it requires you to be genuinely present in that moment with them. As they share the things that matter to them, spend some time realistically thinking about them and see how you can apply their courage, their motivation, or their interests to things in your own life.

If they talk about a musician they enjoy listening to, go online and listen to some of their music. If they tell you about how they grew up watching a sports team, try to watch a game of theirs and learn a little bit more about that sport in general. If they tell you that they are into cruelty-free makeup, try to learn more about what cruelty-free means and how you can adopt a more cruelty-free lifestyle as well. Taking on a piece of what you learn from someone else is a good way to try and step into their shoes to better understand who they are inside. The more you discover about a hobby, interest, or passion of theirs, the easier it will be for you to bring that topic back up for discussion with them in the future.

The next time around, though, you'll have something meaningful to say about it. As you share your own perspective on the experience, you can reflect on it together to see where there is overlap and where there are differences. When it comes to what we know, our own minds are always limited. We've only had so many experiences and interacted with so many people; it can therefore be hard sometimes to see things outside of the bubble we've lived in. Meeting and interacting with new people expands that bubble and helps us see where there are opportunities for us to change our minds, perspectives, beliefs, and interests.

And while this can be applied to all aspects of your life, it's important to make it part of your social sphere, because as you introduce diversity of thought into the equation, you will build a stronger sense of self—which will make you more comfortable with challenges and better able to stand up for the things you say without feeling like you are making empty statements. This is a problem sometimes when you talk to someone you like—your mind can go blank, and you may scramble to find something to bring up that will connect you to them to prevent the situation from devolving into a complete and awkward mess. When you're open to learning, though, you can change that mindset to really being curious about the world. At that point, asking someone lots of questions changes from you doing it to fill in the gaps of silence to you really trying to expand what you know.

Plus, there is a genuineness to the whole experience. The last thing you should ever want is for someone to mischaracterize you as being sleazy. No one wants to open up and share with someone who clearly has ulterior motives. Even if you're head over heels for the person you're talking to, they will see that your interest doesn't lie in just moving the conversation forward, getting their number, and asking them out. It's all about building solid communication and a healthy relationship.

FOR EVERY REJECTION YOU GET, TALK TO TWICE AS MANY PEOPLE

If everyone you talked to just played along and was nice, then it would be so much easier to talk to people. Walking right into conflict is not something that anyone would willingly do. That is why it's so hard to face the uncertainty of rejection from someone you've built up in your own mind to have a higher sense of value than you do. Putting someone on a pedestal can be a process that happens over years. You may know someone for so long and have deep feelings for them but fear the idea of approaching them in a romantic way because you see it as a gamble as to whether the two of you will be able to revert back to the way things were before if the romance part just doesn't end up working out.

The process can also happen the second you see someone. Thoughts may come racing into your head about how they're probably too busy to talk to you or they really would have no interest in communicating with someone like you. No matter how long you've known them, there may be a black hole of defeat waiting in the darkness if things go horribly wrong. That's why you're going to shine a light on that darkness. You're going to expose it, not as a powerful force, but as a moveable object. **You can't stop rejection from happening, but you can stop it from stopping you.** As you push yourself to take small steps in expanding your socially interactive reach … for every person that rejects you, use that as an opportunity to talk to two more new people.

That would mean that if there is a guy you've been crushing on at work but never had a conversation with beyond work-related topics, and when you try asking him to hang out he rejects you, then you see that as an opportunity to find two more people at or near your job to spend time getting to know. Will the sting still be there? It's possible. But the key here is to reduce how much it stings by not putting so much emphasis on how hard it is. You can dilute the rejection by spinning the experience into an opportunity, and with those new opportunities, giving yourself the freedom to redeem that rejection. It's never about ignoring the rejection, it's about understanding it and transforming it into power. As you continue to meet new people, you'll see that some of them will grow to like you as a friend or as a potential romantic partner, and others may just fizzle out altogether.

When we put too much emphasis on one person, we elevate their value to the point where their acceptance or rejection of us seems to be incredibly important to how we go on. It doesn't have to be that way if you're willing to recognize that all of us are trying to navigate this world as best we can. Your crush, no matter how popular, attractive, or successful they may be, is still figuring every day out. If you double up the people that you interact with, being rejected will just seem like a natural part of life. You can reflect on each rejection to understand it, but ultimately you should recognize that it is just one response in the many that are yet to come.

What do you do then if you keep getting rejected over and over? If you're on somewhat of a rejection streak with people, that could be an amazing opportunity to pause and see where you may be going wrong. Analyze how you start conversations, what you say to end them, how you follow up, what personal stories you share with them, and how you lead into being romantic. It's all fair game to analyze, and with more experience in talking to people and in being rejected, your outlook will become more fleshed out and honest because you'll have the experience on which to base it.

CHAPTER 6

Building Confidence

"IN ORDER TO SPEAK WHAT YOU REGARD AS THE TRUTH, YOU HAVE TO LET GO OF THE OUTCOME. YOU HAVE TO THINK, 'OK, I'M GOING TO SAY WHAT I THINK. STUPID AS I AM, BIASED AS I AM, IGNORANT AS I AM, I'M GOING TO STATE WHAT I THINK AS CLEARLY AS I CAN. AND I'M GOING TO LIVE WITH THE CONSEQUENCES NO MATTER WHAT THEY ARE.'" –JORDAN B. PETERSON

SPEAK UP WHEN YOU FEEL LIKE SOMETHING IS WRONG

There will be times in your life where you will come across something that rubs you the wrong way. It might make you feel uncomfortable, nervous, scared, angry, or confused. Whenever you're in a situation that you don't want to be in, your fight-or-flight response kicks into gear and tells you that you should do something, but you might not know exactly what. If it's a fight response, that might turn into you vocally expressing yourself, letting all of your emotions out on the table—or maybe even turning physical by hitting, throwing, or smashing something. If it's a flight response, you may jump into high gear and head on out of there without a thought about what you're leaving behind as long as you make it to a place where you feel safe.

Either way, what we come to see is that the situation we encounter triggers our response. This can mean we end up in a more reactionary mode than a proactive one. How you react, though, may be the best short-term solution you can come up with in the moment—even though it may not be the solution you would want to rely on if the situation happened again. So then what should you do to determine what the right response is? What if you're in a situation against your will and not of your choosing? What should you do to make it through that hard moment in life? Leading with our confidence in a way that feels right to us is how we can carry out our ability to speak the truth. Confidence is also something we can actively build up day by day, starting with speaking up whenever we have the ability to do so.

Each and every single person has a voice that carries its own experiences. It may not always be easy to express ourselves in a way that fully articulates our experiences and shares our perspective of things in a clear and concise manner that people can understand. Building confidence takes time and practice, so first let's explore what a confident person looks like and see what it takes to replace self-doubt with self-worth. When you think of a confident person, your mind may immediately jump to someone who is great at everything they do, who never makes a mistake, and knows how to figure out any kind of troubling situation on the fly. In comparison, we generally see ourselves as a far cry from this confident ideal. Maybe you make mistakes at times, maybe you're not the best at some things, or maybe you panic or freeze up when you're in the spotlight and people are waiting on you to solve things.

It can be easy to doubt ourselves, or even worse, compare our level of confidence to the levels we see others displaying. You might be thinking, *Why do so many people move through life with ease, and yet somehow it's so hard for me to just get by?* The truth is, people aren't moving through life with ease. Everyone is experiencing where they are for the very first time, every second of every day. We don't know what tomorrow may bring. It may end up being something fairly close to what we experienced today, or it might end up being insanely different if just a few major components get changed around. When you first enter high school, you have no clue what it means to be in high school—you haven't lived that reality yet. And that's a process that will stick with you till the end. You're always exploring uncharted territory. Some people are better at pretending than others, but no one has the foreknowledge to be aware in advance of what is to come.

Why, then, are there confident people who can walk into situations as if they do? Where do they amass the strength to challenge themselves as if they already know everything will be OK? To feel more confident about our steps forward, let's take a step back and look there. Take a moment right now to think about the toughest moment you've ever encountered. You don't have to dive too deeply into it, but just recognize what it was for you and hold on to that thought.

When you were in that situation, you might have felt hopeless, like there was no way out of it, and that surely those circumstances were the tipping point for what you could handle. However, here you are reading this book right now, trying to embrace your awkward and improve yourself. That tough moment you thought about has passed, it's not here right now. You've walked away from it, and now you're living to experience another day with a story to tell. The thing is, we're experiencing moments like this every single day whenever we make a decision. Some decisions are big while others are small, but we take on life's challenges constantly, and each day we start again.

Confident people are those who can stand up to the unknown. They put themselves out there to either be carried safely to shore or dragged out and drowned by the sea. If it is the former, then they can reaffirm their trust in their own ability to anticipate what is to come. If it's the latter, then they are willing to accept their defeat and see it as an opportunity for them to be more open to seeing what they missed the first time around. Nothing is static in a confident person's life, they are always seeking new opportunities as a way to better themselves from where they are right now. A major part of that is living your truth and standing by it like you have its back and it has yours. You can come to know your truth only by testing it and seeing what you can learn when you get the results back.

PRACTICING CONFIDENCE

To look at an example of how this might play out in the real world, let's say you're walking on your college campus heading to your next class when you notice a girl sitting on a bench by herself reading a book. All of a sudden, a guy walks over, sits next to her, and starts talking to her. You continue walking to class, half observing what is going on with them and half paying attention to where you are walking, when you start to see the girl giving signals to the guy to leave her alone. The guy, unwavering, continues to sit there with her trying to get her attention as she takes more obvious actions to brush him off, like taking out her phone to look busy or just simply ignoring him. In that moment, you might be hoping that the guy will just take the hint, but for some reason he starts to get annoyed with her and maybe even a bit aggressive in how he's talking to her because she's not paying attention to him. In a moment like that, what does your mind tell you to do?

Response 1: You may feel the need to speak up when you feel like something is wrong, to walk up to her and ask if everything is OK, or even to let the guy know to leave her alone altogether.

Response 2: You may think it's not your problem—why get involved in someone else's business when it has nothing to do with you? They're both mature enough to work the situation out themselves, and because of that it's not worth your time.

Response 3: You may want to interject but don't believe you have what it takes to say what you want to get the result that you want. Because of that, you try to ignore the situation and pretend that nothing is wrong.

It's hard to say exactly what the right response would be, but what does each say about your level of confidence in handling the situation?

If it's the first response, you believe in your ability to make a difference when you see something isn't right. Maybe in talking to them, you find out it's a big misunderstanding and then you can go about your day and not worry about it. No harm done.

The second and third responses may seem to approach the situation differently, but the end result remains the same. You rationalized that seeking out the truth was worth less than not doing so. The desire to speak up fell silent because you thought you didn't know how to even approach the situation, and at the risk of doing it badly, you decided not to do it at all. Now, this example is just a simple one. Life very often gives us tons more variables to work with and potential responses from which to choose. But the purpose here is to really take a moment to think about where we choose to put our confidence on display versus where we choose to back down from seeking the truth due to how uncomfortable it may end up being.

As you practice speaking up in different areas of your life, you'll start to see that it's a process that gets easier. When I was in the tenth grade, I was a quiet kid who barely spoke in class. It wasn't so much that I didn't know the material, I just didn't want to raise my hand and answer questions, because I didn't want to draw attention to myself on the off chance that I would say something stupid or wrong. I wasn't willing to speak my truth even though what I said could have been right, and that left me in a place of pure silence. One day, my teacher pulled me aside after class and told me that there are no wrong answers to any questions as long as those wrong answers lead you in the direction of the right one.

After that day, I decided to test the waters by raising my hand to answer a question he asked in class. I got that first answer right, and it felt good; I felt like all that time I had been holding myself back from confidently trying because I was afraid of looking stupid. And then the second time I raised my hand that week, I got the answer wrong. He smiled at me, told me that I was on the right track, and then explained the right answer to the question. I looked around the class and realized that no one cared. That realization was even bigger for me than the first one ... I learned that my confidence didn't have to rely on others to back it up or even on me to always get things right, but instead on the fact that I spoke my truth, was willing to revise it, and moved forward with what I gained from the experience.

There will definitely be times when speaking up may seem like the scariest step to take and when doing so will completely change your world as you know it and you won't know how to deal with it. But that's exactly what building confidence is all about—realizing you have what it takes, and really taking in the fact that the hardest steps of your past didn't stop you from getting to this moment. It is also realizing that each step is part of your path, building layer on top of layer until your foundation is solid and you can speak your truth from a place of honesty and openness with a vibrancy and willingness to grow in any direction it may lead you.

KEEP ON LEARNING NEW THINGS & LEARN TO LET OLD THINGS GO

•

"HUMAN BEINGS ARE WORKS IN PROGRESS THAT MISTAKENLY THINK THEY'RE FINISHED."

–DANIEL M. GILBERT

•

There's only so much time in our lives to learn everything that we want to learn. We need time to sleep, eat, travel, socialize, and take care of the many daily tasks that pop up, so spending time learning something new is often the first thing we put aside when we try to prioritize our own rat race. As you get older, this may feel more and more apparent to you. You'll look back at your younger years and wonder what you did with all the free time you had, comparing it to today, where it feels like every second of every day is focused on just getting by. In fact, in those moments where you do take some time to try something new, it can feel good in that moment, but most likely, you'll slowly phase it out or integrate a smaller, weaker version of it into your already packed daily routine.

If I'm describing you, then you need to make a change immediately. If what I said made you stop and think *Hey, that's not me*, then you're in luck, because this pitfall can still potentially happen and learning how to avoid it ahead of time will be very beneficial for you. This isn't to say that people are lazy or lack ambition, it's to say that we prefer comfort over discomfort, and sometimes we'll avoid uncomfortable things because it may mean challenging or even changing all that we've known. Realizing that we don't have all the answers and that there's always room to grow is the first step in building the confidence we need to trust ourselves. If a person thinks there is no room for them to improve, then what they will end up displaying is not confidence but arrogance. Falling into a place of arrogance is easy if you never allow yourself to be challenged, or you assume that the people you surround yourself with don't quite understand things to the degree that you do.

It's important to recognize that your experiences are different from others', so the conclusions you draw may have a different arrival and departure than others'. When we interact with other people who have their own perspectives, we have the ability to widen our frame of knowledge simply by hearing them out and genuinely listening to them. The more we listen to others, the more stable we make the conceptual ground around us. We then know that when we approach a topic or a conversation, we will have a better understanding of what's being discussed and how to talk about it in a way that creates the most productive conversation for all involved.

The concept of a "straw man" is when you intentionally misrepresent someone's point and then try to refute the point that you've misrepresented. A straw man is the weakest form of an argument that you can build because it is a manipulation of the truth, and when you sacrifice the truth to give the appearance of winning, you poison the possibility of others growing to trust you and open up to you in the future.

However, the concept of a "steel man" is when you listen closely to what someone else is saying and try to build the strongest case for their position. You listen to what their experience is like and you aim to understand the facts behind their points, and from there you can compare what they say against your own knowledge in order to walk away with the best understanding of all sides. When it comes to building confidence, approaching the world with the openness to learn will rely on your ability to be open to being wrong at times, no matter how defeating that can feel. To avoid arrogance, we have to accept this position, not just so we can be overall smarter people, but so that we can function in the world and aren't tearing down the walls around us.

Your confidence can only be strengthened in this way once you realize that the pursuit of knowledge will carry you farther than sitting up top thinking you have it all figured out. Sometimes, though, it can be difficult to admit when we're wrong because we don't like people to see us as beneath them. We fear that their arrogance may come out, so it can be much easier to deflect, deny, or denounce others entirely. But as I mentioned before, our time is limited, and when we realize that the structure that we built isn't as solid as we wanted it to be and may be in need of repair, reconstructing it can seem like a daunting task to undertake. However, the truth is that it's perhaps the most important task we can take on. We only learn and grow if we're willing to let go of the old. If we sacrifice preconceived notions and constructs that no longer fit within our reality for updated and innovative versions that include the new things we've learned, that is how we can come to walk through life with a sense of confidence that can't be shaken. **Our confidence is built on the will to know, not on what we know.**

TESTING YOUR CONFIDENCE

In the various areas of your life, you will be called to put your confidence on display and tested in a variety of ways. For example, let's say you are working at a job that you feel doesn't pay you what you think you deserve to make. Along with the pay, you also don't feel like the level of the work you are doing is challenging enough for you, leaving you bored on most days and thinking about all the other things you could be doing with your time. What does confidence look like here? For the average person, they may see their semi-crummy situation and justify it by saying, "It's decent enough pay ... I'll just enjoy the weekends ... and at least I don't have to do too much." There ends up being a lack of confidence in their ability to push harder—they think they've reached the top of where they should be and that's where they will stay.

However, if you look at the same situation and tell yourself that you will confidently pursue what you know to be true and you are willing to sacrifice the old to make room to learn new things, your work could change drastically. The first thing you will see is that a conversation with your boss is in order—that you should let him know the work isn't challenging enough and that you believe you could be doing a better job. To "steel man" that thought, you should explain to him that you're left with a lot of downtime and it makes you feel unhappy and unproductive. If you were to take on more responsibility and prove your worth, you could also

> negotiate how you should be compensated for that as well. Your confidence will push you to a new higher level than what you were resting on before, all because you didn't allow yourself to settle for being too comfortable.

To keep it all in perspective, though, pushing yourself to capacity is not ideal either. Sometimes we may feel that downtime is wasted time, and that if we could only do more, then we would maximize our lives and be useful in this world. While this may all sound good in theory, in practice is can actually become more destructive to our long-term existence. Thinking that you're superman is letting your ego carry you to arrogance. We need downtime just as much as we need to push ourselves. Without downtime, we can't properly reflect on what we're doing and determine if it's giving us the type of results we want. There's a world of difference, therefore, between being productive, being helpful, and being meaningful.

Being productive means you're able to accomplish various things. You have figured out how to maximize your output in ways that allow you to do it consistently and with the least amount of error. The only piece that is missing from this is the human element. Humans are prone to error and burnout, so our "maximum productivity" will most likely end up being far less than what our minds tell us it should be.

Being helpful means you're able to work with someone else to get something done. This can sound pretty simple on the surface, but working with other people requires compromise and adjustment. You may need to take the lead at times, and they may as well. Where a problem can occur in aiming to be helpful is when you never are able to stand on your own two feet, when your sense of being starts to merge into the background and your voice becomes less powerful when it comes to functioning outside of your helpful state.

Being meaningful means you're able to cause a ripple effect of change wherever you go. You aim to actualize a sense of good that helps the most people and leads to lasting change in others, who can then pass it on as well. Where meaning can get lost is in the practical application of the idea. Having a goal of implementing meaningful values will still require a plan of action, so if your mind doesn't get past the dreaming stage, you may never get what you want off the ground.

All three of these abilities have to be utilized together in order for us to be our most confident selves. We need to be productive but not to the point of failure; we need to be helpful but not at the sacrifice of our individuality; and we need to be meaningful but not wait until our vision is perfect to act on it. If we can practice these three states, we will feel more confident in our ability to persevere.

Take a moment to think about the areas of your life where you may lack confidence. Do you find it hard to open up to others and accept the idea that they may know something you don't? Are you preventing yourself from really being challenged by the best of all possible ideas so you can build on what you already know? Can you work with others while still standing on your own two feet and actually deliver on what you say you intend to do? These are all questions I want you to take time to think about. Once you do, you will see how your confidence level has changed from where it stood before.

BE THE BEDROCK THAT OTHERS CAN RELY ON

•

"LIFE IS A GIFT, AND IT OFFERS US THE PRIVILEGE, OPPORTUNITY, AND RESPONSIBILITY TO GIVE SOMETHING BACK BY BECOMING MORE."

–TONY ROBBINS

•

Strength is a characteristic that can be defined in a number of ways. There's physical strength—a person's ability to provide protection from the dangers in the outside world that may harm you. There's supportive strength—where someone can take care of your financial needs and offer you the security of a warm home, food on the table, and things to help keep you entertained. And there's emotional strength—the kind where a person is there to listen and offer guidance, kindness, and love when you feel the need to be heard and comforted by someone who cares about you.

Each of these different kinds of strength is important; they all play significant roles in how we grow to care about one another. Giving to another using these forms of strength requires both give and take for the people involved. Practicing both sides allows you to better understand the other perspective. In being open and vulnerable, you're able to see what love and care looks like. In being loving and caring, you're able to see the vulnerable side of others if they're willing to show that to you. A lot of people carry the belief that they don't need anyone else, that life is something they can manage all on their own. In some cases, that's the only choice they have when they don't have family, friends, or loved ones to turn to. This can also be the case when the people you do have to turn to in your life aren't fully there to offer you the support that you need, even if you're willing to offer it to them.

Let's just be real about it, the world is in major need of help. Everyone everywhere is looking for someone to be the person who will stand up and make them feel safe, and who will show them that it's possible to be courageous, move forward triumphantly, and learn in the moment of doing. There aren't many role models to follow, and because of that, so many people are left feeling like they have to go through life alone. Throughout this book, we've talked about understanding who you are so that you can become the person you want to be. And even if you're not a person who feels that you can lead, I would beg to differ, and I'll show you how. There's a few questions I want you to think about first. Each of these questions are indicative of what it takes to be a real leader for others. Before you start to doubt your abilities, keep in mind that when I started sharing my life advice online, I didn't see myself as a leader either.

At first I thought I was just going to make videos sharing my thoughts for my friends to watch. I couldn't see how anyone who didn't know me would care about anything I had to say ... I was just a random stranger on the internet, talking about things for which I wasn't an expert and didn't have a college degree. However, from the first, the things I talked about came from the heart. I shared how I felt and used the internet as a way to help me think through my ideas. Because of that, I continued to grow and evolve. My ideas became more fleshed out, with more structure and a wider sense of the facts that supported my beliefs and my understanding of the world. Have I got it all figured out? Absolutely not. But the questions I want you to think about are ones that I spent time thinking about myself, so here they are.

QUESTION #1: ARE YOU WILLING TO BE A GOOD ROLE MODEL BY GETTING YOUR ACT TOGETHER?

When it comes to leading, people will look at the way you carry yourself daily. Take it from me—this doesn't mean you're under a microscope or have to be "perfect," but it does mean you have to live by a set of values. How you define those values is up to you, but having a set of values that you can stay with is what's crucial to developing confidence and good leadership skills. When it comes to laying out your values, I would recommend considering those around you and how you see them fitting into your world space. For example, do you want to live in a world where you can't trust anyone? If not, then you value openness and should work on demonstrating that you can be open with others. Or let's say you want to live in a world where harm is reduced as much as possible. You may want to look into a vegan lifestyle, where you eliminate unnecessary suffering caused to sentient beings. Identifying your values and working to live by them will mean changing some of the ways you do things now. Having a strong sense of values will make you a good role model for others and will demonstrate that it's possible for anyone to stand up for what they believe in.

QUESTION #2: ARE YOU ABLE TO HELP OTHERS REALIZE THE LIMITLESSNESS OF THEIR OWN POTENTIAL?

This question can seem kind of tricky because you aren't in control of someone else's realizations, and you can't make them believe in themselves. However, you also have the ability to support someone at a key point in their aspirations, which can at times have a far greater impact than if you were to walk with them every step of the way as they work to accomplish their goal. Have you ever had one of your own dreams crushed? Has someone ever come to you with an idea still in its beginning stages, looking for approval or direction on how they should start? Sometimes we can look at things and just naturally tear them down because they may seem ridiculous to us. But a great leader knows that they have the power to help others see that it's OK to ask questions, it's OK to challenge your own ideas, and it's OK to go back to the drawing board. Knowing how to communicate in a way that demonstrates the type of mindfulness and loving-kindness we've talked about in the past chapters will not only empower the person with whom you're talking, but it will strengthen your own patience and character. We all possess limitless potential. We can achieve wonderful things if we only come to realize that as long as we're alive, we can change the world.

QUESTION #3: DO YOU WANT TO TEACH OTHERS THE THINGS YOU'VE LEARNED TO HELP CREATE NEW MENTORS?

It may feel like a huge undertaking to even consider teaching others to be leaders, but it's a long-term idea that should definitely be part of your goals. As you make your way from student to teacher, you should know that the most important step a teacher can take is to inspire a new generation to carry forward the aspiration to be leaders themselves. Carrying yourself in a way that upholds your own values and helping others feel empowered by what they do can only lead to their looking to you for inspiration and guidance as they also find their path and purpose in life. Knowing that your story is important and worth passing on should help give you the strength you need to stay the course. There will be moments of doubt or hopelessness, but remember, there is always someone out there who needs your physical, supportive, or emotional strength. I know you have it in you to show that to others and to in turn open yourself up to receiving help from others as well.

Building up your confidence is so much more than just doing whatever you want whenever you want. There's a discipline in having tremendous strengths and knowing how to properly use them ... that's what makes someone truly confident. Anyone can gain power and force others to succumb to their demands—that's arrogance at its finest. That's why it's up to you to find the proper balance to it all, and to recognize how to be powerful and how to help others with that power. Life really is all about working together and helping each other succeed, because when we are first starting, we need to see people who can tell the truth, who are open to learning, and who offer the foundational support to help us grow. As you walk your path of self-discovery and self-improvement, remember how special you truly are, and never forget it for a minute.

CHAPTER SUMMARY + EXERCISES

In this chapter, we looked at confidence from a different perspective than how most people are used to seeing it. Generally, confidence is seen as a way for you to go after what you want despite the obstacles that stand in front of you. While that may be a piece of it, an even bigger piece is being able to act in accordance with what's important. Acting confidently but without direction can lead to disastrous results like hurt relationships, a cycle of lying, or just a lack of care for the importance of people around you. We talked about how confidence can quickly develop into arrogance if it goes unchecked, which is why it's important to think about the life direction you want to take to prevent yourself from falling into a state of arrogance.

The activities listed below are small tasks you can incorporate into your daily life to help you better outline your path and purpose so you can stay on track with how you want to live a meaningful life. If you aim for the highest good, then you will know that you are doing all that you can to be a role model for others and are living in a way that you can be proud of. Balance will be the key, because if you get stuck in over-analysis, you may become paralyzed by choices and be afraid to make a move for fear of judgment, criticism, or rejection from others. The most important thing to remember when trying to accomplish these tasks is that failure is not enough to hold you back. Failure is sometimes part of the learning process. So if you can accept that, you may not always do these things flawlessly, but will try your best to walk the middle ground of recognizing that you're not perfect, but you are great.

STICK TO TELLING THE TRUTH FOR A DAY, THEN A WEEK, THEN A MONTH

When you tell the truth, you have far less to worry about because the only story you have to stick to is the one that actually happened. Most of the time, when we tell a lie, we are eventually met by chance with someone challenging us on that lie and even catching us in it. With lies, you have to think about the details that have been bent to fit the new narrative, remember how to tell that story again and again in case it resurfaces, and worry about the potential of becoming branded as a liar by others. Once you get caught in a web of lies, the trust that others hold for you can easily be diminished. They may start to feel that there isn't a reason to open up to you, because if you can't tell the truth, why would they ever want to rely on you to keep in mind an accurate and honest depiction of what they share?

•

"IF YOU TELL THE TRUTH, YOU DON'T HAVE TO REMEMBER ANYTHING."

−MARK TWAIN

•

The way to eliminate all of these problems is to aim to stick to the truth. At first, simply try to do this for one day. Telling the truth doesn't mean being brutally honest or offensive, but it does mean sharing how you feel about things and living in alignment with what matters to you. Let's say someone invites you to hang out after class or work that day and you feel really anxious about going because you have things you have to work on. Rather than committing to something you may not enjoy just to be courteous, try telling the truth by letting them know that you don't feel comfortable going that day but that next time you may feel differently. Or let's say you're asked about rumors or gossip about someone you know. You don't know the full details, and you don't know how it may end up affecting the person you heard about, so telling the truth in that case might be choosing not to spread anything that could be false. It can be hard to deal with different types of situations in which you may be under social pressure, but aiming for the truth is one thing that you can stand by no matter what anyone else says.

Try doing this for a day, then a week, and then a month. Make it your goal to be transparent and honest while being kind in how you speak. Far too often people use the idea of "the truth" as a way to hurt others or to speak without regard to the ripple effect of their behavior. The truth can have a positive effect with everyone with whom you speak, so do all you can to prevent it from being warped by others' nosiness, anger, or resentment. The more and more you end up telling the truth, the easier you'll find it to maintain your path of enlightenment. You will no longer carry the burden of lies with you; instead, you'll be free knowing that whatever comes your way, you will offer real, genuine, and honest advice as best as you can.

SIGN UP FOR A SOCIAL ACTIVITY

Working toward a more confident you is going to require you to step out of your comfort zone from time to time. In order to make real change, you're going to have to take small steps to get there. What each person considers large or small can definitely vary; however, one thing that everyone should do just to make sure they hold themselves accountable is to sign up for an activity that has a social component to it. You may ask yourself if that's possible for you to do, if that's too big a step for you to take, or if you will even be ready for it when the time comes. Before we get into those questions, though, here's how you can really decide on an activity to focus on and how you can organize your priorities to motivate yourself to make time for it.

As you work on building your confidence, how will you ever really know if you're making progress without actually putting it to the test? It's incredibly easy to become an information junkie ... to spend your time reading books, watching YouTube videos, signing up for online boot camps and courses, and even talking about all the things you're learning without actually bringing them out into the real world. By committing yourself to something where what you've learned will be showcased for the world to see, you will end up being more committed to actually accomplishing your goal. Let's say for example that you've always wanted to learn a new language, but you've put it off because there's no need for you to do it at this exact point in your life. You might keep nudging it to the back of your to-do list, and even when opportunities present themselves for you to display what you know, you may start to feel that you lack the confidence to do it properly. The fear of failure becomes magnified, and because of that, your dream of learning a new language goes nowhere.

But let's say you decide to commit to learning a new language, and you want to find a way to really stick with your goal. If you were to sign up for a poetry or storytelling contest where you had to speak that new language, even just looking ahead at the date and time that you will be performing creates a sense of commitment. You're locked in—it isn't just an idea in your head or something you aspire to do. It's something that people will rely on you to do, and there are a lot of people involved in creating the space where you can succeed. As time passes and you get closer and closer to the performance date, you'll feel the push to step up your game, take things seriously, and try your best. But what happens if you arrive on the performance date and you're not at the point where you want to be? Well, you go out there and make the most of it.

Success isn't determined by how well you do here, it's determined by your ability to move forward into uncharted territory by doing something that you could never have imagined doing just few weeks, months, or even years ago. After you experience this once, doing it again for another activity will be easier because you'll have broken the inertia you had imposed on yourself. You can forge ahead knowing that trying new things (and maybe not being good at them right off) is all part of the learning experience, and that sometimes you need to jump into the pool to learn how to swim.

People make this mistake all the time when they sign up for the gym. They get a membership and feel that determination to go in the beginning because it's new and exciting. But because they don't have a set goal to work toward, they eventually start to slack off. I know what you may be thinking ... *wanting to lose weight or get ripped* is *a goal*. The difference, however, between a goal you want and a goal you commit to is how real you make it. So what are you waiting for? What is something you want to feel more confident doing? Find an activity connected to that goal and commit to it. A few months from now you'll look back and thank yourself for making it happen.

CONTACT ONE OLD FRIEND A WEEK AND LISTEN TO THEIR STORY

There's always a million things going on in your life, so making time to stay in touch with people can be a real challenge. Whether it's scrolling past an old friend's picture on Instagram or "liking" a classmate's status on Facebook, we frequently interact with people in passing. There often isn't enough time for meaningful in-depth interactions, so we settle for short, bite-sized communication and move on with our day. And while this does increase our ability for us to know a little more about a far greater number of people, the quality of the relationships we maintain tends to falter in the process. In fact, things may even get to a point where interacting with people with whom we rarely interact feels awkward, foreign, or just not like something we would really even want to do if given the chance to talk to them in real life.

Have you ever had an experience like this? I mean the kind of moment where you see someone who you haven't seen in a really long time, but you still choose to avoid talking to them because filling in the gap since you last interacted is far too much to cover in the brief amount of time you'll see them now. In my opinion, this takes a toll on our confidence. It puts us in a position where we aren't excited about strengthening connections but instead feel relief and comfort when we can avoid them. For this task, the best way to prevent this mindset is to choose one old friend every week and reach out to them to catch up. Dedicate the time needed to really connect with them again; show them that you want to know how they have been and that you miss what the two of you used to share. There are two major benefits that can come from reconnecting. The first is that you are practicing your skills of starting a conversation with someone. It challenges you to think about what you two have in common, to find those overlap points, and to improve your ability to be more personable.

The second benefit is that it makes the other person feel special. One thing I've talked about frequently is our desire to feel loved by others. Knowing that people care about us and think what we have to say is important is what drives us to open up to others in the first place. Plus, you may end up discovering that the two of you have grown in ways you would never have imagined. There are lots of people who come into our lives for only a short while, but we hold on to them because we feel curiosity about what they're doing in their lives. By reaching out and connecting with them, you can display a level of confidence that goes beyond security. In some cases, you might even find out that you and that person have grown in completely different directions, which can also lead you to be more open to letting them go.

Communication is the underlying method to use to determine who may be worth your investment of time. Those you can communicate with are worth keeping around. There's something of value to be shared with them, whereas with people with whom you can't communicate, by letting them go, you'll be avoiding spending your time in places that don't serve your growth. Overall, see it as a way to strengthen your bond with your current friends rather than as a way to cut people off. Once you get into the mode of wanting to eliminate people, you'll become much more selective when it comes to who is worth your time talking to. Build your confidence so you can approach, open up to, and listen to anyone you encounter. Know your limitations, and pursue relationships of value and meaning. That's how you're going to create trust in your ability to accomplish the goals you choose.

CHAPTER 7

Embracing the Awkward

"YOU RARELY HAVE TIME FOR
EVERYTHING YOU WANT IN THIS LIFE,
SO YOU NEED TO MAKE CHOICES. AND
HOPEFULLY YOUR CHOICES CAN COME
FROM A DEEP SENSE OF WHO YOU ARE."

–FRED ROGERS

LIFE IS WHAT YOU MAKE OF IT

We all have different struggles to face; some of those struggles lie behind us, some we're dealing with right now, and others we've yet to even consider. If you're ready to embrace the awkward that lies ahead of you and want to truly succeed at school, life, and your relationships, then you have to be able to give yourself a break. Throughout this whole book, we've talked about stepping up and getting out there to challenge yourself as much as you can. When you really make the effort to do that, you're going to see monumental changes in your life. You'll have open communication with the people you interact with, you'll pave the road that leads you to doing what you love, and you'll trust in your ability to manage the stress, anxiety, and failure that comes along with all of it.

Most importantly, you'll learn to be patient with yourself and cut yourself some slack.

We put too much value on the little passing moments we experience, and even sometimes feel like those moments are infinite and we'll never be able to escape them. Often, we forget that other people are also dealing with challenges and most likely aren't judging us as severely as we're judging ourselves. I know it can be easy to criticize yourself for not maximizing every opportunity you have or to beat yourself up over something you should have done better. I've done that all too many times in my own life as well. Over the years, though, I've grown to develop a new type of relationship with awkward moments. When I was younger, I felt that there was nothing I wanted more than to escape them at all costs. Once I escaped one, I would frequently replay it in my head and think about being back in that situation, only more in control of it and fully confident in my ability to handle it.

I remember back in high school when I was dating my very first girlfriend. At the time, I was super awkward and shy. I didn't know what it meant to be in a relationship or how to be a good boyfriend. I had the courage to ask her out, but everything after that was a new experience for me, so I spent a lot of time in my own head wondering what might be the right move to make. This happened to me all the time with her. I would feel awkward when we would walk together, wondering if I should hold her hand or put my arm around her. Even when I went to kiss her goodbye after walking her home, I didn't know how long the kiss should be or how I could go into it in a way that was suave and smooth. I never stopped to take into account that she too was experiencing those feelings in her own way for the very first time. And instead of sharing how I honestly felt and working with her to manage that situation together, I just dove deeper into it.

There was one time in particular when the two of us were going to hang out at her house by ourselves after a half-day at school. From the moment we got there, I froze up and didn't make a move at all. I wanted to kiss her, to put my arm around her, and just to just enjoy the experience for what it was, but instead I let the awkwardness take over, and it kept me in my head once again. It wasn't until later that day after I said goodbye to her—and she had that hopeless look on her face which screamed out disappointment to me because I hadn't made any effort at all—that I spent the whole walk back to my house thinking about all the things I had wanted to do. *How did I mess it up? Why did I freeze up? Why was the whole situation so awkward for me?*

I had lots of questions and probably always will, but what I learned from that experience was that when you are in those moments of uncertainty is when you need to embrace the awkward the most. Had I taken a moment to breathe and practice being mindfully in the present, I might have been able to remember that we were sharing that experience together. Either way, I learned a valuable lesson from that experience, one that helped prepare me for what was to come in the future.

While I was still in college before I got my first internship, I planned on potentially becoming a police officer. My father had sold me on the idea of it being a solid and stable job and one where I could work for twenty years and then receive my pension. I was a little unsure at first because I didn't think police work was something I wanted to do, but I eventually decided to just try it out and see where it took me. Step by step, things seemed to be working out in favor of me being a cop. I took the psychological test and passed it, I set up an appointment for the physical exam, and I even did the personal evaluation with the police force to see if I had any history or past record that would bar me from getting the job. Yet every time I took a step forward, I felt like I was getting more and more locked in. A feeling kept rising to the surface telling me to speak up and say something, but I just didn't know how to address it. I found myself sitting in the police headquarters with my awkward feelings, unsure about making the decision but not determined enough to call it all off.

Because I had invested so much time and energy into it, I felt like I couldn't back down at that point. The idea of failing at something I had put so much time into made me think everything would have been for nothing. My parents would be disappointed in me, the police would be disappointed in me, but most importantly, I would be disappointed in myself. I had never taken the time to really think about what I wanted to do. Had I invested time beforehand into discovering what my strengths and weaknesses were, I would have seen that I wanted to help people but that doing it with a badge was not my style. I also should have just asked for help; if I had spoken to more people who were police officers, I would have gained a much better understanding of what would be required of me before I took the long road to that point.

Speaking up when situations were awkward wasn't always an easy thing for me to do. With new experiences, there are always opportunities to second-guess yourself. It is easy to find excuses to avoid doing things the way you instinctively wanted to handle them. That's the natural learning process sometimes ... which is why it's so important to prepare yourself with the skills that will allow you to embrace what lies ahead. I ran into a situation like that when I was ready to propose to my wife. We had been together for several years, and yet the thought of proposing to her terrified me. I wasn't so much afraid that she would say no, it was more that I feared the idea that the proposal, the ring, and the time and place just wouldn't be up to par with what I thought she was expecting. For a while I kept beating myself up, not sure what type of ring to buy because I felt like she wanted me to just somehow *know* what to get her.

The fear of failure had really begun to beat me down. Every time we talked about marriage and the possibility of me proposing, I would tense up and fall back into that awkward place where my fear of disappointing her and being rejected clouded my mind entirely. I felt like no matter what I would do, it just wouldn't be good enough. And yet, these weren't feelings that I verbalized, so it looked like I just didn't care enough to go for it. This went on for a long time—the two of us remaining in the cycle of her waiting for me to act and me waiting to feel confident enough to do it. Eventually though, push came to shove, and I had to make a decision. I asked myself what was important to me and realized I had to make the commitment and move forward (despite it not being perfect) or risk losing the opportunity and the girl along the way.

I decided it was finally time to act. I talked to her about the type of ring she wanted, and after some back-and-forth deliberation about the style, the stone, and the color, she made her choice and I ordered it. When the ring finally came in, I knew things were real now. There was no turning back in my mind. I had to put all my previous efforts to learn new ways of doing things to the test here: being more mindful, overcoming my fear of rejection, recognizing that I might fail, acting with compassion toward myself if I did, and confidently asking her to be my wife so the two of us could move into a happy and healthy life together. When the day finally came, it was our fifth anniversary of being together, so we decided to spend the day in Manhattan to see the Christmas tree in Rockefeller Center and then eventually the tree in Bryant Park. When we moved over to where the tree was, I knew I was going to go for it. All the old fears had taken over me again, but in that moment, I put myself through the same exercise that I've described to you: compare yourself to where you were before. I thought about how I had taken small steps forward. and now here I finally was.

I stood in front of the tree with her (a moment which I'm sure she was expecting at this point), got down on one knee, and asked her to be my wife. I wanted her to know how special she was to me and how important it was for me to do this. I don't think she quite understood the awkwardness I had been feeling the whole way through, but when she said yes, it washed it all away for me. Things seemed right with the world. I had embraced my awkwardness and realized that life really is all about what you make it. No matter how troubling the situation may be, there are *always* small steps you can take to find your path to success.

BE PROUD OF WHO YOU ARE AND WHO YOU WANT TO BECOME

•

"SUCCESS DOESN'T COME FROM WHAT YOU DO OCCASIONALLY, IT COMES FROM WHAT YOU DO CONSISTENTLY."

–MARIE FORLEO

•

While it may seem like the most obvious thing in the world to say, there really is no one in this entire world quite like you. You may have rolled your eyes reading that (I know I did the first time I heard it, too), but even if you feel like it's something super cheesy to say, it's important to remember that it's true. There's no one in this world who has had the same experiences as you, the friendships, the highs and lows, the mistakes and the successes. You really do walk a path that no one has ever walked before, and the crazy part is no one else ever will.

And yet, for some reason, we sometimes find it easier to downplay our uniqueness. We think we're nothing special compared to the other students in our classes, the other people with cultural similarities, the other citizens of our country, or the other humans on our planet. Why do we sell ourselves short? The fact that you're one of a kind is something to celebrate. It means you have a way of seeing the world that no one else has. There's a power in being proud of who you are, in knowing that you can contribute something positive and meaningful in this world, because whenever you do, it's always in your own individual way of doing so.

There will be times in your life when expressing who you are in the world will feel incredibly awkward. Seeing someone else celebrate their successes is difficult for a person who is struggling, so people may be quick to tear you down just to show you their belief that if they can't achieve what they want, you shouldn't either. No one likes a gloater, a show-off, a bragger, or a pretentious know-it-all. You can pick any name under the sun for it, but all of it comes back to one thing: insecurity. When you're climbing the mountain and aiming for new heights, you will encounter people who want to drag you down. Their insecurity will prevent them from seeing their own potential for growth and shift their focus over to yours. They will study your every move, waiting for you to slip up just so they can take that chance to rub it in your face.

But just like we talked about before, failure is not final. You're going to fail again, maybe today, maybe tomorrow. It's what you do *after* you fail that defines you, how you learn from your errors and change for the better. You may not be entirely proud of who you are right now, though; you may feel there's a lot of work that needs to be done before you'll get to a point where you can be happy with yourself. If you're waiting for the right time to tell yourself that it's OK to be you, there is no better time than right now. There is no job title, career path, or action you can take that will somehow make you worth caring about. You're acceptable just as you are, with the good and the bad that you carry.

When I decided to really focus on making videos, I encountered a lot of backlash from my friends, people I thought were supposed to be supportive of me. I was still figuring out how to get comfortable in front of the camera, so the way I spoke, acted, and portrayed myself came off "fake" or "scripted" to some. I had friends tell me that my channel was too boring to watch or that I was too goofy to take seriously. It was incredibly hard for me in the beginning to record new videos every week knowing that the small audience that people like me have in the beginning—our family and friends—didn't think what I was doing was serious. I kept telling myself that as time went on, my videos would get better. I would learn what my style was, I would get into my groove, and I would be able to make my focus less about how I acted on camera, because how I acted would simply be a portrayal of who I actually was.

And that's when YouTube banned me from making money using their platform. I didn't understand how ads really worked at the time, so when I got the notice, I just ignored it altogether and kept making videos. This was something I loved to do, and I knew that if I couldn't figure out a solution for how to make money from my craft right now, I would figure it out later. It wasn't until two years later that I started to get more traction with my videos. I started to see comments from people asking questions about life, dating, my thoughts on what was going on in our culture, and what my philosophical beliefs were about things like religion and more. I was starting to really know what I wanted to do, but there was a nagging feeling that knowing how I would actually turn my hobby into something profitable was still out of reach for me.

There was no one I could talk to at the time because I just didn't feel safe opening up to my friends. The same friends who had mocked my content before were the last people I wanted to ask to help me figure out a solution. Luckily, at the time, I was able to connect with a YouTube Multi-Channel Network which helped me set up my ad revenue just around the time my channel started to pick up. I had hope that this was finally going to go somewhere—that I was actually making it now despite what all my detractors had said. It was one thing to not like my style of content, but looking back, I could see that the responses I received were from people who wanted to hold me back. There wasn't support there from them because they hadn't had support when they were reaching for their goals, and now that someone else was finally succeeding in their own way, it was something they just didn't want to see happen.

Even now, after making videos for years and years, similar thoughts still come across my mind: *What if they're right? What if what I'm trying to do won't amount to anything? What if I'm just not original enough to stay relevant? What if my channel gets demonetized and*

I'm forced to find other ways to support it? Trying to deal with those internal questions was difficult, mainly because of the stumbling blocks I had encountered on my journey so far.

Sometimes it can be challenging to let go of your past, especially if it's riddled with regrets stemming from your old ways of thinking. But the first step toward change can happen as soon as you're ready to take it. Your life is the sum of every experience you've had, twisting and shaping to bring you where you stand. What you have in front of you is the chance to look at past mistakes and to see how they've hurt you, but also strengthened you. You have already lived through what has passed, so learning from the past should keep moving you upward, not backward.

When I was younger, I did a lot of things I regret; if I could go back in time, I would completely change how I handled them. In middle school, I remember being a bully to other kids because I had been bullied myself. I felt like it wasn't fair that kids would have fun at my expense. They would make me the butt of their jokes, and they would rag on me for not having the coolest clothes or for simply not being a part of their groups. It made me feel so much less than them, so as a way to redirect my hurt, I went ahead and did the same thing to kids I felt were lower than me. There was one kid in particular I would pick on just because he was awkward and shy. At the end of my eighth grade year, I ended up finding out who he had a crush on and devised a plan to get his yearbook and make him think his crush was going to sign it, only for me to write something really dumb and mean in it.

I thought it was the funniest thing in the world at the time. Looking back at it, I feel incredibly embarrassed and ashamed of what I did. After a bit of convincing, despite him already not liking me, I told him that I would bring it to her to sign since he was too scared to talk to her on his own. When I walked away with it, I wrote down my mean message, brought it back to him and laughed about it with my friends. The kid was completely distraught; he felt deceived, hurt, and I think most of all, powerless ... the same feelings I had felt when my bullies had bullied to me. Now I was just as bad as they were.

What experiences in your life do you look back on with regret? I mean the type of moments when you know what you were doing wasn't the right thing to do, but you decided to do it anyway. I could choose to look back at that moment as something I want to erase, or I could try to pretend that it never happened to ultimately attempt to erase the trauma and pain I caused that fellow bullying victim in my eighth grade class. If I just moved on with my life, wrote it off as no big deal, and pretended that everything was fine, then it would probably be fine, right? Not really. It is not helpful to look at regrets this way, as it doesn't lead to any growth.

When I think back to that story now, I see it as an opportunity for me to prevent the same thing from happening to someone else. I know what I did was wrong, and I know how easy it can be to justify our own wrongdoing. We just simply write it off as no big deal. And while sometimes the bad things we do are small-scale, other times they can really impact the course of someone else's life in the worst possible way. That's why we need to look at our own misdeeds—no matter how hard it may be to relive those past memories—and tell ourselves that it's part of the story of how we got here. Also, we need to realize that from this moment on we can do better. We will do better. For our own sake, the sake of the people we care about, and for the sake of the people's lives we've yet to change.

IT'S OK TO LAUGH, EVERYTHING IS TEMPORARY

•

"A MAN WHO BECOMES CONSCIOUS OF THE RESPONSIBILITY HE BEARS TOWARD A HUMAN BEING WHO AFFECTIONATELY WAITS FOR HIM, OR TO AN UNFINISHED WORK, WILL NEVER BE ABLE TO THROW AWAY HIS LIFE. HE KNOWS THE 'WHY' FOR HIS EXISTENCE, AND WILL BE ABLE TO BEAR ALMOST ANY 'HOW. ' "

–VIKTOR FRANKL

•

By now you should have it all figured out. Everything you need to know to succeed in life is shrunken down into this bite-sized book.

If only things were that easy.

What I hope to have helped you figure out, though, is that you don't have to back down or give in to the struggles you face. You can face them head-on by working with the people who love you and by realizing that it's going to take time to bring your best self to the forefront. Most of the time, people tell you to work on being yourself, that just acting on what comes natural to you is the best way to handle what you encounter, but I don't think that's true. The reason why I focus on helping you be your best self is because there are always things you can work on. So as long as you aim for the highest sense of good possible, you'll constantly discover new perspectives, feelings, and outlooks on life.

Now, I know your journey might seem a little different from the misconceived path of just waking up one day with that *aha* moment and drastically changing everything you've ever known. But you've got real-world issues to deal with. You've got to worry about things like keeping up your grades at school, finding a job that doesn't chip away at your soul, making a relationship flourish with someone you really like, and even coping with the suffering of losing a loved one. Like I said, real-world issues. The major problem I have with "self help" advice is that it sort of exists in its own little box, with tips and tricks that if done in the right systematic order, will leave you with nothing to worry about moving forward.

Or at least that's what seems to be implied. But we both know that's not true.

In fact, when I think about applying the guidelines I've mentioned in this book, I fall short of keeping to them all the time. I'm not always in the moment when someone frustrates me, I don't always feel like I know exactly what my path is, and I certainly don't always feel confident when I talk to people. And the interesting thing is ... it's totally normal to feel that way! You don't have to have it all figured out right now; this is a lifelong process you learning as you live. It's small steps from here on out. Every. Single. Day.

I remember back in high school, I had this one teacher who was a bit quirky. He was always wearing a suit to work, he would hum to himself before the students came in, and he was very meticulous about watering his classroom plants. In that class I was pretty shy ... I only spoke when I had to, and I really tried my best to blend into the background, despite all of us having our desks set up in a circle around the room.

One day he wanted our class to go over a poem that I had never heard of before called "The Secret," by Charles Bukowski. The title alone intrigued me, but what he had us do first was each read the poem individually to ourselves, and then he went around the room and had us read it out loud. I remember the fear clenching up in me as it got closer to my turn, but when I finally read the poem out loud, it just felt like a bunch of random somber thoughts meant to leave the reader feeling hopeless. I want you to read the poem yourself and take a moment to think about what it means:

don't worry, nobody has the
beautiful lady, not really, and
nobody has the strange and
hidden power, nobody is
exceptional or wonderful or
magic, they only seem to be
it's all a trick, an in, a con,
don't buy it, don't believe it.
the world is packed with
billions of people whose lives
and deaths are useless and
when one of these jumps up
and the light of history shines
upon them, forget it, it's not
what it seems, it's just

another act to fool the fools
again.

there are no strong men, there
are no beautiful women.
at least, you can die knowing
this

and you will have
the only possible
victory.

When the class finished their read around, the teacher had asked us what we thought it meant. Someone said it sounded like the author was depressed. Another student said it sounded like someone who had been hurt before. Different people chimed in to give their own interpretations until the teacher shared his perspective; he said that he saw the poem as being hopeful. I was pretty thrown back by that ... what was hopeful about this poem at all? From there, he explained that he felt the author was actually being sarcastic, and that he was making a point to show how easy it is to be cynical, but how important it is to remember that we have the choice of how we want to carry our lives forward in this world.

I looked back down at the poem, reread it to myself, and realized that it actually did seem quite sarcastic to me. I ended up silently laughing to myself, thinking no one had really noticed, until the end of class that day when the teacher came over to me to talk. He asked me what I thought about the poem we'd read, and I explained how after hearing a different perspective on it, I realized it was possible for me to carry the optimistic interpretation of it even when the text itself had never changed.

Life is sort of like the poem. We always encounter moments that are in need of our response. Sometimes, those moments can completely freeze us in our tracks and leave us feeling immobilized by their awkwardness. Finding a way to embrace the awkward is all about allowing yourself to change your perspective, despite what the circumstances you face are. Yes, there will be things that are beyond your control that can affect your life completely. But you have the power over which markers of success you want to achieve, whether that's something big like running for president to inspire hope in the world or petting your dog's belly after a long and strenuous day.

Figuring it all out is part of the journey of life. What I've tried to outline here are just a few of the steps you can take to help make that path clearer for you. You won't always get it right, nor will you always know what to do, but allowing yourself to make mistakes and learn from them is the real teacher of life. I'm confident in your ability to succeed because I know you're willing to open yourself up to learning. There are so many people in this world who are struggling with that step alone. They take every move so very seriously, never wanting to look weak or out of sync with the way others perceive them. They're afraid to laugh at themselves simply because it might invite the opportunity for others to laugh at them too.

Don't beat yourself up. The only standard you have to live up to is your own, so craft a life where your standard is solid enough that it will not only help you succeed, but also help the people you surround yourself with to rise. People also have this fear that somehow the things they do and the decisions they make are permanent. You become a deer frozen in the headlights because the wrong move might signal your end. I know, because I've been there plenty of times before. This can look like holding yourself back from saying yes to something you really want to do, choosing the safe and easier path instead of the challenging and exciting one, or keeping your feelings to yourself because it's easier to just accept the things that other people do to you.

Decisions are temporary. For most of what you'll encounter in your life, you'll see that choosing choice A over B is hardly ever permanent. Sure, you may not have access to option B anymore, but picking your first choice will lead you to a whole new set of choices to make. So no matter where you are right now, if there's something you want to do, something you feel so strongly about that you can't imagine a world where you don't pick that option, push yourself to go for it, but don't get tripped up thinking the decision means life or death. As long as you are alive and breathing, there is room to reflect, room to grow, and room to change the world once again.

Laughter can be a way to help you manage the struggles you face when you're trying to find the right path for yourself. When you're able to laugh about something, you remove the shield you keep around that issue to make it untouchable. If you try to practice mindfulness in your own home but you're constantly bothered by people trying to grab your attention, laugh about it, and realize that you can approach that situation as a chance for you to open yourself up to others, rather than seeing it as you not being able to get into your zone. If you work up the courage to talk to someone you have a major crush on and then in the last second you freeze up, laugh it off and put your confidence on display with someone else around you.

You give yourself the chance to suffer less by seeing the moment as temporary, one that will not define you forever as a person but instead as something that you can laugh and smile about. We can manage what we take in from others if we're able to peacefully laugh about its impermanence. Things may be important, but not so important that they can break us down. Finding the right balance between stepping up and putting your all into something as well as with being OK with it not working out is how you are going to overcome any awkwardness that arises. To truly embrace the awkward, we have to be willing to accept the possibility for change with open arms and a willingness that isn't tied to the views of others. Once you can start to do that, you'll find that the resistance to discovering who you are will start to become clearer and clearer. The pieces will fall one after the other, almost as if they were placed there on purpose by someone or something greater than you.

So take a moment to really think about what lies ahead for you. Look back at your own experiences: the struggles you've overcome and how hard you've worked to get to where you are, and the people who have guided you and been there for you, the ones who have seen you at your worst and have proudly stood by you at your best. Take a moment to reflect on all that you have become and all that there's still left for you to do. Because there really is so much more to accomplish, and the world needs people who are willing to compassionately, mindfully, and confidently lead us. This goes far beyond me and anything I could ever share with you. It all comes back to you and all the potential you possess.

There is no door too heavy for you to open, there is no person too different for you to connect with, and there is no opportunity that is too important for you to either choose or decide to walk away from it. Your real path of success rests on what you want and what you're willing to fight for. So fight for what's right, set an example for others, and let them know that you have a purpose, that you're willing to be your best self, and that you have what it takes to embrace the awkward and truly be somebody great.

As always, love and peace.

ACKNOWLEDGMENTS

I want to take a moment to thank each and every one of you for reading this book. I know sometimes listening to advice isn't easy, especially when there is change that comes with it. I'm happy you've made it this far and I hope that you'll use the ideas shared here to find your own unique and special way to work towards improving.

I would like to thank my mother and father for giving me the structure and openness to discover the answers to things on my own. To my dad, who showed me that curiosity and kindness are essential traits for discovering what you love, and to my mother, who showed me that being a leader is a duty, one that you must embrace if you have the potential for it.

I also want to thank my wife, Kseniya. She always has my back and is always there to help me when I get too sucked into the world of creating. Without her, I would most likely forget to eat, forget to sleep, and forget to take my eyes off of the computer screen. Thank you so much for keeping me alive.

There have also been so many influential people along the way who have really inspired me to grow as a person. My brothers, my friends, and pretty much everyone I have ever interacted with. Looking back at all the experiences

I've encountered throughout my life, it really puts my journey and how I got to where I am in perspective. Thank you, everyone, that has shared a piece of your life and story with me. You've helped me shape my own life into something I am truly grateful for.

And finally, reader, I would like for both of us to take a moment to think about all of the people who have loved us into being. The people who have helped you become who you are. Those who have cared about you and wanted what was best for you in life. Acknowledge them, remember them, and make them proud.

ABOUT THE AUTHOR

Joshua Rodriguez is a motivational speaker across multiple digital platforms including YouTube, Snapchat, and Instagram. He has built a mass following of middle school and high school teens looking for advice in different areas of their life: self-worth, relationships, academics, and family. His videos and content have been featured in prominent marketing publications and also been used in many different schools across the country. Josh has also been a guest speaker at many schools across the east coast, where he teaches the values of compassion, mindfulness, and confidence.

Josh was born and raised in Brooklyn, New York and has worked in education technology, "ed-tech," since college, communicating with teachers, principals, and students. Josh's teaching approach is inspired by Fred Rogers, who taught children that feelings are mentionable and manageable, and Thich Nhat Hanh, who speaks about being in the here and now by cultivating peace in every step.